How and Why to Read an Children's Digital Books

How and Why to Read and Create Children's Digital Books

A Guide for Primary Practitioners

Natalia Kucirkova

First published in 2018 by
UCL Press
University College London
Gower Street
London WC1E 6BT

Available to download free: www.ucl.ac.uk/ucl-press

ISBN: 978-1-78735-349-7 (Hbk.)
ISBN: 978-1-78735-348-0 (Pbk.)
ISBN: 978-1-78735-347-3 (PDF)
ISBN: 978-1-78735-350-3 (epub)
ISBN: 978-1-78735-351-0 (mobi)
ISBN: 978-1-78735-352-7 (html)
DOI: https://doi.org/10.14324/111.9781787353473

Contents

List of figures

Preface

This textbook was commissioned to accompany 'Children's Reading on and with Screens', a short professional development course co-developed by UCL and the National Literacy Trust. The course was designed for UK primary school teachers and includes face-to-face training and online learning content. Although completion of the course requires students' engagement with this textbook, the book is also a standalone resource for an international audience. It will be of particular interest to existing or aspiring teachers (student or trainee teachers) and educational professionals. Librarians and policy-makers, educational researchers, and developers and providers of digital reading content for children may also find the book a helpful resource.

The textbook is published electronically, as well as in print, and therefore has some features characteristic of electronic format. For example, self-directed content exploration is encouraged with embedded hyperlinks to cited resources. To ensure the textbook is suitable for an international audience, it was important to ensure that the text was written in a straightforward style without complex or rare vocabulary and that technical terms or acronyms were defined and exemplified. Thanks are due to my publisher and reviewers in helping me format the content according to these requirements.

Throughout the textbook, I recommend various online resources. Researchers need to be cautious about translating findings into practice given the amount of replication and verification necessary to make claims of efficacy and effectiveness. At the same time, researchers who work closely at the intersection of practice and design – as I have done over the past years – recognise that parents, teachers, educational professionals and community workers seek solutions and practical ideas, rather than statements of complexity. Digital books and apps are already in children's hands, the genie is out of the bottle, so to speak, and practitioners want to guide children's choices. In light of this reality, I make several suggestions in relation to approaches and resources that

[handwritten margin note: This was my 1st question.]

practitioners might find suitable. There are two big caveats that I invite all readers to consider before adopting a resource or approach. First, the digital books and apps on the current educational market have not been evaluated by a body of work that can prove their effectiveness. It is very unlikely that a straightforward use of an application or a reading program will significantly improve the complicated and complex process that is a child's learning. Similarly, my examples of other teachers' approaches may be suitable for the context of these teachers, but they may not fit another learning environment. It is only the combination of a measured approach with suitable components that can, over time and consistent application, bring about noticeable positive changes. Therefore, I emphasise again: at this stage of research, it is difficult to say which particular approaches, let alone which particular resources, may be considered effective. My aim with all the recommendations I make in this book is to provide useful suggestions that could be considered appropriate. My choices were guided by the socio-cultural theoretical framework, which emphasises the role of adults in mediating children's learning experiences with tools and technologies. You, the reader, make a significant difference to how a recommended resource might be used or designed with the children.

The second caveat regarding my recommendations is that many digital media are commercially produced and behind a paywall. I have no financial or commercial interest in any digital books, apps, web services or other products mentioned in this book. (I was actively involved in the development of the *Our Story* app, which has always been offered for free.) In selecting the recommended resources, I drew on my experience of using them with children, teachers and parents in my work, as well as their personal recommendations. The world of digital content is dynamic and products appear and disappear on a daily basis. It is plausible that by the time this book reaches you, more and newer resources will be available. It is also possible that you will come across more suitable story-making applications or digital library systems that work better in your context than the ones I recommend. If you believe the resources you use in your classroom may be relevant for other people please let me know and I would be happy to review them for future iterations of this book. It is also possible that over time some of the hyperlinks that I have included in this book will no longer lead to the intended resources. If this is the case please let me know and try searching for the resource with its name. If the resource is still available but associated with a different hyperlink, the online search should bring you to the right place. If when reading this book you discover some important omissions or oversights, again please let me know. The big advantage of digital books is that they can be revised more easily and make use of collaborative and pooled knowledge. I can be contacted via email at n.kucirkova@ucl.ac.uk or Twitter @NKucirkova.

The power of stories

The stories we tell each other reflect an astonishing richness of individual and shared histories and anticipated futures. Digital technologies have changed the ways in which these stories are communicated and received. Children respond to these changes with curiosity and without judgement. They grow up surrounded by stories represented in films, books, games, and their friends' and family's words, body movements, facial expressions. These different representations feed off and feed into each other. I approach reading for pleasure in the broadest sense, which includes making meaning of written words, and pictures, manipulating the printed or digital book, and using all one's senses to interpret the story.

Children's reading on and with screens can involve reading comments from their Minecraft co-players, practising phonics skills with literacy apps or enjoying Harry Potter on an iPad. Unlike adults, today's children are unconstrained by a history of being limited to printed books and the habits that have developed as a result. So long as the story interests them, children enjoy engaging with the story characters in paperbacks or hardbacks, in an augmented-reality app version or via a Kindle e-book.

The role of teachers/educators and caring parents is crucial in this age of technological change. We all carry the responsibility to ensure that children are exposed in their reading to diverse formats as well as content. Reading on screen offers unprecedented access to diversity but also unprecedented means of reducing this diversity through targeted algorithms. Children's discernment in navigating the reading landscape is essential. Cultivating this discernment is a lifelong journey for communities of readers. I suggest one way of starting this journey: positioning children, teachers and families as co-creators of the texts they engage with. I conceptualise such reading in terms of agency and reciprocity.

[handwritten margin notes: Double edged corn → same as ≠ to develop cheap to sell]

Agency and reciprocity

[handwritten note: MUCH MORE COMPLEX LANDSCAPE]

Agency is a fundamental characteristic of human beings; it is the volitional choice we all have for thinking and feeling a certain way. Johnston (2004) describes agency in relation to how teachers make the classroom environment responsive to individual children. In education, agency is about feeling empowered and competent to think and act. My aim with this textbook is to encourage children's and adults' agency in authoring their own stories and digital books. Any valuable agency can be asserted only within the framework of reciprocity. Reciprocity is about belonging and the dynamic and ongoing process of negotiating a shared perspective and calibrating responsive relationships. In this textbook, I focus on reciprocity between authors and readers, between adults and children, as well as between reading and writing and between reading on screen and off screen.

Agentic reciprocity connects to the conversational nature of reading and the dialogic self, topics that have been richly theorised and researched by my academic colleagues. I refer to these works throughout this book and provide some specific suggestions for how, within such a theoretical framework, digital books can be used with young children. The reciprocal negotiation between personal agency and shared communities can be illustrated as an 'ARC', as captured in Figure 0.1.

Digital books

are teachers? up to this?

The primary school is a unique context in which to encourage, strengthen and extend children's reading on screen and off screen. Children bring to school the stories they have heard, viewed or read in their communities and the reading habits they have observed among their family members and friends. As such, each child is a storyteller in waiting. However, far too often, the richness of children's personal stories and the diversity of children's contemporary reading experiences go unnoticed and unrecognised. In large-group school systems, it is up to teachers and other professionals to take up the mantle of modelling and supporting children's personal stories and children's expression of stories through reading and writing.

Placed alongside the documented decline in book diversity (Ramdarshan Bold 2018) and some reports of fluctuating motivation in children to read print books (e.g. Common Sense Media [2016] in the US and National Literacy Trust [2016] in the UK) and in students to read long literary texts (Baron 2015), it

Figure 0.1 Agency, reciprocity and community.
Source: Author

HOW AND WHY TO READ AND CREATE CHILDREN'S DIGITAL BOOKS

is it route to reading for pleasure?

may be that story-based digital books enriched with interactive features could invigorate children's motivation to read for pleasure.

With digital books, children whose first language is not English, and children with language difficulties, can access stories via embedded multimedia and interactive features. Children can also listen to the stories and get immediate feedback or help when they don't understand. Story apps can be programmed to read to the child, with highlighted text and hotspots that link the story text to specific points of interest. This may be a useful feature in environments where there are not enough teachers for large classrooms or in families where parents are missing because of illness, distance or conflict. What is particularly valuable with digital books is the participatory nature of digital texts. Children can participate in conversations about their reading with other children accessing the same digital library or digital text. Digital books also open up the space for story authorship by offering multimedia options. These spaces need to be enabled and enriched by the expertise of teachers, librarians, parents and researchers. In this textbook, I summarise some key research insights to deliver ideas of practical relevance to educators and other adults who support children's reading experiences. I focus on digital books created for, with and by individual children and call such books and the reading they support 'personalised'.

Personalised reading and me

Personalised reading and innovative approaches to supporting children's reading have always fascinated me. I began my research with personalised print books, which we co-created with parents using paper, scissors and cut-out pictures. When tablets and iPads appeared on the market, I was intrigued by the possibility of creating a personalised book in a more seamless and polished way. I have led the development of a smartphone/tablet app called *Our Story* which was designed to support parent–child story-making. To understand how such self-made digital books can be used among diverse populations, I have worked with teachers across the globe (in the UK, US, Spain, Japan, Malta and Slovakia) with typically developing children as well as children with complex educational difficulties.

I continue to explore practical developments in the area of children's reading on screen and working closely with app developers and children's publishers in designing new products. There are three guiding principles in my work: that children's reading needs to be personalised to intrinsically motivate them; that an optimal reading diet needs to incorporate multiple media, formats and genres; and that children's reading needs to be reciprocal and mediated by others to be of lasting value. In my design work I call these principles 'Personalise–Connect–Share'.

There are various ways in which the process of Personalising–Connecting–Sharing can be facilitated in homes and schools. In this book, I focus on story authorship and story-sharing. I explain these processes in a more detailed way in scholarly works concerned with agency and reciprocity in reading (see Further Reading). In my conversations with teachers and families, I explain these processes with the 'baking metaphor'.

book making

The baking metaphor

I love baking and it was when I was making one of my favourite almond cakes that I thought of the analogy between mixing flour, eggs and sugar and mixing text, audio and images in children's stories. I have been using the baking metaphor with teachers in my workshops for years; I fully describe it in an article for teaching professionals (Kucirkova 2015c: https://www.childcareexchange.com/catalog/magazine/). The metaphor is simple: in terms of ingredients, digital stories are made of images, sounds and text. Stories look and 'taste' different depending on how these ingredients are mixed together, in which quantities and who sources them from where. The more the child is involved in 'baking' the stories, the more they are likely to appreciate the final result but also the role of the individual ingredients in it. Importantly, cakes are to be shared and recipes are to be tried out and exchanged, which is an important analogy to be considered with children's multimedia stories. I enjoy baking cakes because they can be shared with others and create a nice moment; similarly, multimedia stories can be used to create a positive atmosphere with our loved ones as well as with people we don't know.

You could perceive this book as a collection of recipes and ingredients for baking and enjoying children's digital stories. I have done a lot of work with teachers experimenting and testing and through this process we've learnt a lot about our own tastes and others' preferences. Nevertheless, the suggestions for activities and examples of resources that I share in this book are unlikely to satisfy all tastes. Remember that good bakers are those who can use recipes creatively to satisfy their guests with the ingredients and tools they have available. It is my hope that the insights presented in this book will advance your culinary skills to satisfy the reading habits of children you care about.

Acknowledgements

There are many people who have helped me with the creation of this book; I name only a few of them here. First and foremost, I would like to thank my publisher, UCL Press, for supporting this book and making it freely available online. Open access is an important means for the democratisation of reading on screen. I am pleased and honoured that my book can be part of the educational movement that aims to create freely accessible open learning spaces.

I would like to acknowledge the input and contribution of my colleagues at the UCL Institute of Education who volunteered to be advisory board members for the 'Children's reading on screen' course. I would also like to thank our collaborators from the National Literacy Trust, who shared many constructive suggestions. I gratefully acknowledge the help of the UCL Life Learning Team in helping us to conceptualise and realise the short professional development course 'Children's reading on and with screens', which this book accompanies.

Finally, my thanks go to all the children, teachers, parents, librarians, publishers and designers I have worked with over the years. Their enthusiasm and stimulating ideas inspired me to research children's reading on screen and I owe them all my biggest thanks.

← The baking metaphor is a clear way of understanding the complexities of on screen texts.

1
Introduction

[handwritten note: 4 components frame that story]

Aims of this textbook

There are four key concepts that frame stories and the 'recipes' for making them: process, product, format and content. In terms of *process*, this textbook focuses on stories that support children's reading for pleasure. That means that I describe story ideas and story-making apps that are designed to support children's enjoyment of stories, motivation to read and identity as a reader. In terms of *products*, this textbook focuses on children's storybooks. That means that I highlight stories captured in writing, images or sound. Stories shared orally are an important predecessor of storybooks (indeed that is how we started sharing stories), but are not the focus of this book. In terms of *format*, this textbook focuses on children's digital storybooks. This means that I foreground stories available on various kinds of screens, including mobile (tablets, smartphones) and static screens (desktop computers). In terms of *content*, this textbook focuses on personalised digital books. This means that the central point of the book is personalisation, and personalised digital books made by children or their relatives or teachers or by librarians or other community members. The content of these stories is determined by these individual groups of people, so the best way to describe it is to say that it is personalised, unique and authentic, to them.

This textbook aims to offer an accessible and evidence-based guide to children's digital story-based books and personalised reading with and on screens, considering these as specific examples of children's contemporary reading experiences. I focus on expanding reading opportunity for children who can read but often don't, not on teaching reading processes. As explained in later chapters, this specific area of emphasis carries great potential for children's learning. The textbook follows this particular focus because of a practical need to provide specific, research-based and practice-verified resources for educational professionals interested in using digital technologies to support children's learning. Although a wide range of materials are available on the use of technology in schools and there are several academic books dedicated to the use of digital media in schools, there is currently no free and comprehensive guide to practical strategies for supporting digital personalised reading with young children. As a freely available resource, this textbook aims to address this gap and provide a guide that is rooted in research and practice with children's contemporary reading experiences.

Who is this book for?

This book is aimed at adults who work with children and guide them in their learning. These adults may be teachers or other educational professionals or adults schooling their children at home or librarians interacting with children in the community. Given the focus on books, apps and learning platforms that support children's learning experiences, the book is also relevant to the creators of these resources, that is, designers and publishers and the policy-makers who oversee and regulate them. Educational researchers, particularly those who work with teachers and are interested in applied scholarship, may find the book a worthwhile addition to their reading list.

The primary audience is teachers because of the crucial role teachers play in mediating children's reading lives. Although publishers and the international market in children's books will continue to push out new trends, and children will continue to adapt to them, the role of teachers in guiding children's reading is critical. (I am not referring to the teaching practice of 'guided reading' here but to guiding as in mediating and mentoring.) Teachers have a significant role in the children's book market. They make an impact on the reading landscape through their participation in book selections and awards and their influence on headteachers' decisions to purchase particular titles. As Hunt (2000) writes, 'what happens in the 21st century depends to some extent on the symbiotic relationship between children's books and schools. How books are treated in education is directly linked to the books that are produced and marketed' (p. 112). Teachers' perceptions and attitudes concerning reading on screen (and use of technologies more broadly) have a critical influence on how and whether screens are used in classrooms (Mathew Myers & Halpin 2002). With digital books the teacher's instrumental role in mediating access and deployment of books and technologies becomes doubly important.

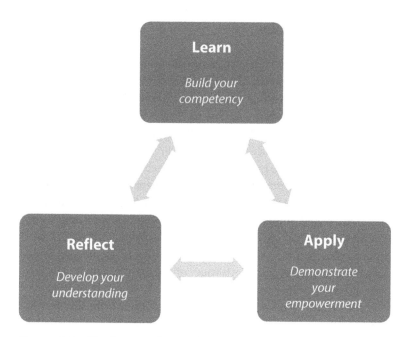

Figure 1.1   The learn, reflect and apply cycle of knowledge and skills development.
Source: Author

The abundance of screens in the home as well as school and public spaces means that children have access to multimedia content all the time. The challenge for teachers and caregivers is to guide children towards content that expands their minds and motivates them to be their best selves. This challenge cannot be solved with a single approach or product. Similarly, there are no research-based practices that can be universally applied in all schools and learning environments: schools cater for children who come from diverse backgrounds. Thus, if there is anything that all schools have in common it is that they are all unique in their own way. To support children's learning well, teachers need to be what Oliver Quinlan (2013) described as 'thinking teachers', who develop their own ways of mentoring their students. I attempt to support this process by including examples that can be adapted to different contexts as well as by linking to research to explain reasons for specific approaches and resources. I hope that teaching professionals and non-professionals will be able to use this material in the cycle of learning, reflecting and applying. The book will thus be able to make a practical contribution to the development of digital reading tools for young children and new ways of encouraging reading for pleasure among young children and the teaching profession.

Space for conversation

Although there is no opportunity to comment directly on specific sections of the book through a forum discussion, I encourage readers to have a conversation about individual chapters or paragraphs and share their inspirational practices with each other. Many teaching professionals are already part of online forums and involved in Twitter and Facebook debates as well as face-to-face groups created through their local municipality or school network. In *The Digitally Agile Researcher* (Kucirkova & Quinlan 2017), contributors describe the many ways in which researchers and any other curious professionals can take part in online discussions. If you are interested in others' thoughts on the topic of personalisation, you could, for example, start a Twitter discussion by suggesting the hashtag #personalisedstories. Or, if the digital aspect intrigues you, you could hold a small discussion group with your colleagues about their views on children's reading with screens.

There are multiple opportunities to branch out from this text to other texts and multimedia resources, which illustrates the interactive and agentic nature of reading on screen. Some chapters of this book aim to prompt your reflection with suggestions in dedicated reflection sections and links to further reading not readily available online. My favourite quotes by famous writers are woven into the reflection sections to stir thinking and point beyond my words. I aim to incrementally update the textbook and enhance it with new practice examples over time.

Brief overview of the textbook's individual chapters

There are 10 standalone chapters in this book, divided into two parts. Part I focuses on existing commercially or empirically produced digital books that have been made by professionals for children. Part II focuses on new and potential digital books that are created by children, their family members, teachers and other significant adults.

The Preface and this introductory chapter set the scene and explain my approach to the topic of personalisation and reading on screen. In this chapter, I provide some definitions for the key terms that frame this book and explain what digital books are, what they look like and where they can be accessed. I also explain and describe the basic nature of personalised reading, so that subsequent chapters can discuss its implications in more detail.

In Chapter 2, I zoom in on a specific facet of children's reading on screen: reading story-based multimedia interactive books ('digital books' for short). I provide a research overview of the promise and perils of children's digital books. The goal of Chapter 2 is to ensure that readers are aware of and understand the limitations of digital and personalised reading and at the same time recognise the strengths and potential of children's reading on screen.

Chapter 3 outlines criteria to evaluate the educational quality of digital books, as well as their potential to support reading for pleasure, children's online and offline reading practices (so-called 'blended engagement') and broader democratic and human values such as inclusion and diversity representation in children's stories. Practical strategies centre on the ways in which digital books can be deployed in the classroom, with some practical ideas of using digital books alongside the English curriculum.

Chapter 4 continues the line of explaining practical strategies for the use of digital books in the classroom with emphasis on supporting children's digital literacies and language and communication skills. Effective strategies with digital books focus on supporting children's independent reading with the 'read to me' feature of digital books, as well as one-to-one, small-group and bigger-group reading of digital books in the classroom.

Chapter 5 outlines how digital books may support individual children's needs, strengths and difficulties. An overview is provided of how the child's age relates to engagement with digital media and with digital books in particular. The chapter provides several examples of digital books developed to support children with language and reading difficulties, dyslexia, traumatic injury, attention-deficit disorder (ADD)/attention-deficit hyperactivity disorder (ADHD) and autism. I foreground the characteristics of individual resources to facilitate adults' decision-making on the suitability of digital books for the children they want to use the books with.

Part II moves away from existing and commercially produced digital books to self-made personalised books. The approach of self-made digital books is broken into three chapters: digital books made by children (Chapter 6), digital books made by parents (Chapter 7) and digital books made by teachers (Chapter 8). Each chapter follows the same structure of explaining first the reasons for the approach and its benefits for the children and reading community, and then how this approach can be adopted by the key stakeholders, with examples of resources and case studies. The key rationale for digital personalised books is that, in creating their own digital books, adults and children can 'reassert the potency of the personal' (Cremin 2016), which is at the core of reading for pleasure and children's intrinsic motivation to read. In addition, given that a personal voice is inherently diverse and unique to each individual (regardless of gender, ethnic background or abilities), self-made books address the issue of diverse reading content by profiling the personal voice.

Chapter 6 details the ways in which children enjoy making their own digital books and the story-making apps and programs that can support this process. Children's story-making grants them multiple entry points into a story. Children's digital stories can be shared with other classrooms or schools and they can also be used to enhance home–school dialogue. The framework of the '5As of personalisation' – that is, five factors that are implicated in personalised learning (authorship, autonomy, authenticity in content, aesthetics and attachment) – are used to explain why and how children's self-made books contribute to their learning.

Chapter 7 positions teachers as creators and co-creators of children's digital books. Teachers' authorship could address the low quality of educational content available for children's reading on screen and could also enhance the ways in which children's digital stories connect homes and schools. Although many teachers have incorporated self-created books into their literacy teaching already, not all teachers have the skill sets, knowledge and technical opportunities to create children's digital books. The chapter suggests approaches and resources to support this process.

Chapter 8 outlines how digital books created by parents could foster intergenerational dialogue in the family, the celebration and preservation of dual language use and positive sharing of digital technologies at home. Tips for approaches and resources to support parents in creating digital books for and with their young children are provided.

Chapter 9 departs from the preceding chapters in that it focuses on book systems and ecosystems rather than individual digital books. Digital library systems can help teachers and children find relevant content, archive readers' responses to individual titles and share these with others on a large scale. The chapter considers the nature of reading supported by digital libraries curated by teachers, with related pedagogical practice and approaches. Underpinned by the view that reading is a social practice, the opportunity for international communities of readers to come together and exchange stories is illustrated with examples of digital reading hubs and digital libraries and reading systems.

Chapter 10 concludes the textbook with a visionary forecast of how children's reading on screen could evolve in the next few years. Attention is paid to current developments in the area of *tangibles*, which are physical toys that connect to digital stories. Together with smart toys that connect children's personal story worlds with commercial producers, these new technologies represent an important shift in children's reading and relationship with stories.

Given that use of smart toys and tangibles is increasingly popular among children, teachers need to be aware of their potentials and limitations. Whether and how these new forms of story-making and story-sharing could enrich children's experiences in the classroom are considered and discussed. In addition, story-infused learning environments, such as those supported by reading charities, are outlined as possible new directions for children's blended story experiences. Organisations such as the UK-based Ministry of Stories connect communities locally and internationally, and through structured programmes empower young children to be story authors and story-makers.

Overall, agency and reciprocity are emphasised in this book as central to the use of digital books designed and authored by children, and adults' mediation of this practice. It is by no means about using children's content for evaluation purposes or collecting evidence to judge children's skills and knowledge.

The book concludes with the reminder that reciprocity in story-making and story-consuming reflects the internal/external dialogue between self and others and is key to a holistic approach to children's stories. Children move fluidly among the multiple ways in which stories can be expressed. 'It is not a question of book or e-book for children. The two can complement each other' (Kucirkova 2014c). This book makes the case for the added value of personalised and digital books in children's reading. This focus can only be justified if we agree that non-personalised and physical books are indispensable to children's reading. Please remember this important point!

Key terms and definitions

It is worth pointing out that terms relating to digital phenomena are characterised by ongoing fluctuations and developments rather than fixed meanings. This is true also for educational practice and research and reflects the novelty of the digital world for all stakeholders. For researchers, terminology depends on the research discipline and philosophy and is therefore not universally agreed. The definitions and terms that I use in this book have been carefully chosen to represent various disciplinary approaches to children's reading on screen, though I recognise that in attempting broader definitions I have simplified terms that are vastly more complex. I also recognise that by explaining new terms I am simultaneously defining them. With this caveat in mind, here are the key terms used in the book and my definition of them.

Children

Now, you might think that, since 'children' is such a commonly used word, it doesn't need a definition. I wish to clarify three points about my use of the word 'children'. First, I refer to young people as 'children' rather than 'kids' because most British educationalists prefer the word 'children'. I avoid the use of 'pupils' and 'students' because they have strong class-room-related connotations and I want to focus on learning in any environment, formal, informal and those in-between the two. Second, I focus in this book on children of pre-school and primary school age. In the UK, this corresponds to children aged between three and eleven years; in international contexts it is typically two to twelve years (see Kucirkova et al. 2017b). The adults supporting these children in formal learning are in the UK called 'pre-school practitioners' and 'primary school teachers'; in international contexts they are mostly referred to as 'teachers' and 'educators'. Third, I feel strongly about not homogenising children as one group: all children have their own needs and preferences. It is purely for simplicity and ease of explanation that I divide up the chapters in terms of typically developing children and children with special needs (Chapter 5).

Reading

As Maryanne Wolf (2018) says, children are not born as readers; it is not in their genes to know how to read. Reading is an active process and involves word recognition (or conversion of graphemes into phonemes) and text comprehension, or knowledge of print and knowledge of stories, as we often say in early education. There are various ways of describing the complex process we call 'reading'. Wolf makes the useful distinction between *deep* and *shallow* reading. This distinction has been used to study the difference in adults' and older children's reading of different text genres (e.g. long literary texts versus bits of news) and modes of reading (on screen versus off screen). For young children who are only beginning to read, educationalists often make the distinction between reading for pleasure and reading for learning. 'Reading for pleasure', also known as 'recreational reading', 'ludic reading' or 'reading for enjoyment', is about children's intrinsically motivated, volitional reading that brings wonder and delight. Special weight is put on the child's intrinsic motivation to read. 'Reading for learning', on the other hand, is more about reading for a specific goal. It captures the process of decoding letters as a means to learning something new. The distinction between reading for pleasure and reading for learning is useful when, for example, designing an app for children's stories and deciding whether to put emphasis on fun stories or teaching children historical facts. The difficulty with the division between reading for pleasure and reading for learning is that it could be interpreted to mean that reading for learning is always a chore whereas reading for pleasure is always fun. In my understanding, reading for pleasure/learning is one way of simplifying the complex process of children making sense of letters on the page. In this book I consider all reading for pleasure to be part of children's learning, but there are some contexts that are more or less conducive to different *types* of learning.

Learning

'Learning' is another problematic term that divides rather than clarifies the relationship between education and entertainment. The term 'edutainment', which combines education and entertainment, has been adopted as a preferred term in the community of technology researchers who aim to ensure that children's engagement with technology is enjoyable as well as challenging and instructive. In selecting the resources and approaches for this textbook, I sought to make sure that they support a range of children's cognitive (language, thinking) as well as emotional and social skills.

Fiction and non-fiction books

Texts read by children fall into two main genres: fiction and non-fiction. Broadly speaking, 'fiction' follows a narrative (a story plot) and contains some story characters; 'non-fiction' contains factual information that may be about specific people (biography), animals, places or events. Fiction and non-fiction texts that are presented in the form of pages that are bound together or connected together digitally are called a 'book'. I use the word 'book' rather than 'text' in my writing to avoid potential confusion with 'text' understood as any story, including films and video stories, or any non-story text, such as a text message. Although some digital books contain moving images, I focus on stories that contain text and illustrations and are more like print books than films. Although news stories and biographies are now widely available for primary children in interactive digital forms through publications like *FirstNews* and *The Week Junior*, I do not cover these. Rather, I focus specifically on fiction.

A book can be printed and contain physical pages and a cover and spine. It has a weight and volume which help readers gauge the book's length. A book can be also presented on a screen. Depending on the screen on which it appears and the particular form it takes on this screen, the book can be an e-book, iBook or app.

E-books and digital books

'E-book' is short for an electronic book that, for children, is typically accessed on a desktop computer or older versions of reading devices such as Kindle 2016 e-readers. E-books present the text as well as the audio version of the text but contain only static pictures. iBooks are digital books specifically designed for Apple devices, such as iPads, iPods and iPhones. iBooks can be accessed only from the iBooks Store, which is a dedicated marketplace for digital books developed for Apple devices.

Children's e-books that contain a fictional narrative are often called 'story apps'. Those which contain a story but represent it only in pictures with no words are called 'picturebook apps'.

In terms of their features, e-books are different from print books because they can be enriched with interactive and multimedia features. 'Multimedia' literally means 'many media' and in the case of e-books includes the media of sounds, visuals and text. 'Interactive' features, as with print books, involve the reader's ability to interact with the book through touch and physical manipulation. But whereas a print book allows physical interaction through page-turning or touching different textures in a board book, an e-book allows physical interaction on the screen. Designers incorporate interactivity into e-books through so-called 'hotspots', which are areas on the book's pages which can be activated through touch. For example, when a child touches a hotspot on a story character, the character can move around the page or change colour. When a hotspot appears on the text, the e-book can define the word or speak it aloud. Interactive features are also used to create small games or interactive activities within e-books. The presence of games/activities in digital books has led some adults to question whether reading digital books with these features still counts as 'reading' or should be described as 'digital play'. My answer is that a native digital book is a hybrid of media and therefore needs to contain features that differ from those of traditional print picturebooks. The unwritten rule among designers is that if a digital book contains more than 70 per cent animation it is considered a game rather than a story e-book or app.

In order to publish an interactive multimedia e-book, designers and publishers need to present it as an application, or 'app', that can be purchased for tablets and smartphones. For tablets and smartphones sold by Apple, apps can be downloaded and purchased from the App Store, whereas for tablets and smartphones sold by Google, apps can be downloaded and purchased from the Google Play App Store. These two stores have some broad quality checks in place that focus on the appropriateness of the material and its general appeal to customers. Both stores also feature users' ratings and comments on individual apps. In addition, the technology providers have developed easy-to-use platforms to generate and create content. However, neither Apple nor Google Play has any content-related criteria concerning the e-books' educational value. The new scale of available content facilitated by online production coupled with the lack of quality control has meant that the current markets for children's digital books are overcrowded and difficult to navigate.

On both the App Store and Google Play, interactive multimedia e-books are sold alongside apps for games, health & fitness, entertainment, dating, food and many other categories. This means that their role of supporting children's reading for pleasure can be misinterpreted or missed. This is one of the reasons why this textbook was written.

'Interactive multimedia e-book' is rather a mouthful, so some researchers, including me, have been referring to these books as 'digital books'. Digital books present stories in visual (illustrations and text), audio (sounds including voiceover and music) and interactive modes. They can be read on any screen and purchased from either of the two app stores.

Having clarified the key process (reading) and resources (books) that this textbook focuses on, I now turn to the word 'personalisation', which you might associate with services such as personalised news or personalised holiday packages but less so with the context of personalised reading with children.

Personalisation

'Personalisation' contains the word 'person', that is, a human being. The verb 'personalise' refers to tailoring something for a specific individual. If the tailoring process involves a group of individuals, it is called 'customisation'. Since customisation is about groups, the content needs to be made relevant for groups rather than individuals. For example, customised books may be books for specific age groups or books relevant for boys or girls. If we use the word 'customise' as a verb, we refer to the process of tailoring generic products according to pre-existing templates and scripts (e.g. the same shoe design can be customised for different age groups). With Mattel's 3D printer, children can customise existing characters based on Mattel's templates and then print them out in different colours.

The process of personalisation differs from customisation in that it does not rely on existing content or design but rather leaves the content or design open to the individual child. For example, personalising a digital book doesn't mean choosing whether it's read by a male or female voice, but it may mean adding the reader's own voice-recording to the story. A fully personalised story can become a personal story, especially if the personalisation process is carried out by the child (rather than by an adult for the child or by the child for another child).

Personalisation is a key means to encourage children's authorship and authentic contribution to the literature discussed and shared in the classroom. Yet, little is known about personalisation supported and led by teachers and children's caregivers; this textbook aims to provide an up-to-date account of the various forms and implications of personalisation in children's reading. Specific focus is placed on digital personalised books, that is, digital books that are created by children, teachers and parents. There are some research projects (see Chapters 6, 7 and 8) and a wealth of online guidance (e.g. Book Trust: http://www.bookstart.org.uk/books/lets-write-a-story/) to support book-making in schools. However, the extant projects and resources focus on paper-based book-making, privileging a traditional print-based and text-focused model of literacy. If we are to diversify the reading landscape and engage all children in reading, we need to include digital personalised books as well.

Personalised reading

'Personalised reading' is reading that is tailored for, or by, a specific child. Personalised reading is an increasingly commercially important area of children's reading, particularly reading on screen. Personalised reading on screen occurs when children read personalised books or access personalised reading systems. But personalised reading can also occur without screens. For example, adults can personalise the content of a book when reading it to the child, by making links between the story characters and the child's life. They can say things like, 'Look, the prince has brown hair just like you have.' Or they can ask questions that relate the story narrative to the child's experiences. They can prompt the child's memories by asking questions like, 'Do you remember when we visited cousin Malcolm and he showed you the walnut tree in his garden? Well, his tree will soon bear walnuts like Cinderella's three nuts. Only hers are magical.' When adults personalise children's stories with such personal links, they increase children's story comprehension, add coherence to their memories and help them recognise patterns in the world around them. In the educational literature, this process has been studied in terms of adults' use of decontextualised and distancing talk (see for example Curenton et al. 2008). What I focus on in this book are personalised reading *products* such as personalised books and reading systems. Although I do not specifically discuss adult-led personalised reading around screens, I hope that readers will consider it in their reading-related practices with young children. Remember that we all can make stories more meaningful and enjoyable to children if we personalise them, whether this is directly by changing the book or indirectly by changing our talk around the book.

Personalised books

Print books are 'personalised' if the text or illustrations contain a personal reference to the child. The most straightforward way to personalise a child's book with a textual reference is to use the child's name for the main protagonist. The child can be the story's protagonist and other story characters can carry the names of the child's friends or relatives. In a personalised book, a child's favourite toys, foods or places can also be part of the story text. A personal visual reference could be a child's own drawing – if the child personalises the book themself – or the child's photograph. One book can contain one or more personalisation markers; the more personalisation features it has, the more it is authentic and unique for the specific child. A digital personalised book can, besides personalised text or illustrations, also contain personalised sounds or voiceovers and personalised interactivity. The latter occurs when readers interact with the story elements in ways that are unique to them – for instance, when they create their own avatars.

Personalised books can be created by children or by adults for children. In this book I focus on personalised books that are self-made, either directly by children or by teachers and parents for children. Personalised books can also be bought from publishers, by teachers or parents supplying the publishers with data about the children. For instance, the publisher Wonderbly Ltd offers various print-based personalised books that can carry the child's name and even a photograph of their front door. Another publisher, Mr Glue Stories Ltd, offers digital personalised books in which users can replace the story character with their own name and add their own drawings or voice-recordings. They can then purchase the digital personalised book as a paperback. The use of children's personal data needs to follow data protection and safeguarding guidelines, as per the General Data Protection Regulation and ethical principles, explained in full by Kucirkova, Ng and Holtby (2017a).

Personalised books for children are becoming a multi-million-pound business as more and more publishers invest in personalised versions of their titles, the most popular ones selling millions of copies worldwide. Personalised books made directly by children and those who love and educate them are a non-commercial alternative, which, as explained later in this book, have significant potential to provide diversity and learning benefits.

Personalised reading systems

While the main purpose of personalised books is to engage children in reading and experiencing fictional narratives, personalised reading systems typically aim to teach children new concepts or provide them with a set of tailored reading experiences. Unlike digital personalised books that are personalised by the user's direct input, personalised reading systems are run by algorithms that automatically generate content based on the user's characteristics or past activity. For example, the personalised reading system iRead developed by researchers at UCL and their European colleagues (see https://iread-project.eu/iread-consortium/ucl-knowledge-lab/) aims to provide children with apps and games that correspond to the child's reading profile and progress with the reading games. If a child struggles with decoding then the system will recommend an app/game that supports this skill and adjust other content the child accesses through the iRead platform. In this respect, personalised reading systems can be thought of as following an adaptive learning model. Such models are increasingly used in higher education online courses and in commercial shopping websites and are also widespread in the design of video games. Their incorporation into children's learning is rapidly growing, although awareness of their affordances among the general population is relatively low. Chapter 9 describes such reading systems in detail and the ways they could position teachers to enrich children's reading for pleasure.

Reading systems are powered by algorithms and relate very closely to the public debate on personalised/programmatic reading and the amount of personal data we share online in return for personalised reading recommendations. Many blame the problem of commercialised and divisive digital content on recommender systems and algorithmic reading. It is true that a lot of harm is being caused by misleading, incorrect and defamatory information propagated online. Societies are only beginning to deal with the consequences of the digital revolution. I do not wish to sidestep these important macro-level considerations, but I emphasise the importance of agency and authorship as one way of approaching online reading. Throughout the book, I encourage children, teachers, parents and other stakeholders to be the agents of change by authoring the content children read and fostering a sense of belonging. This is my small way of contributing to the 'government versus technology giants' conundrum and suggesting a possible model of change.

Chapter summary

This textbook focuses on children's reading for pleasure with digital books and personalised digital books. *Digital books* are defined as story-based books with multimedia and interactive features. *Personalised books* are books created for or by individual children. This textbook focuses on digital personalised books made by children, teachers and parents.

> ## Further reading
>
> Below are some articles and books I have authored or co-authored which connect directly to the themes of personalisation, children's digital books and reciprocity. Not all are freely available, but you should be able to obtain them by requesting them through your library or, if you don't have access to a library, by contacting my publishers or me directly.
>
> Kucirkova, N. (2017) *Digital Personalization in Early Childhood: Impact on Childhood*. London: Bloomsbury Academic. This book provides a comprehensive overview of the area of digital personalisation and children's learning and can be freely accessed from Bloomsbury Open Collections via this link:

https://www.bloomsburycollections.com/book/digital-personalization-in-early-childhood-impact-on-childhood/

Kucirkova, N. (2016) 'Personalisation: a theoretical possibility to reinvigorate children's interest in storybook reading and facilitate greater book diversity', *Contemporary Issues in Early Childhood*, 17(3): 1–16. This article outlines the key reasons for positioning children as story authors.

Kucirkova, N. & Littleton, K. (2017) 'Developing personalised education for personal mobile technologies with the pluralisation agenda', *Oxford Review of Education*, 43(3): 276–88. This article argues for the importance of combining personalisation with pluralisation, which you can think of as a combination of personalisation and diversity.

Here are my four favourite classic texts for everyone interested in reading for understanding, deep reading, reading for meaning and reading for pleasure:

Bruner, J. S. (2009) *Actual Minds, Possible Worlds*. Cambridge, MA: Harvard University Press.

Cremin, T., Mottram, M., Collins, F. M., Powell, S. & Safford, K. (2014) *Building Communities of Engaged Readers: Reading for Pleasure*. London: Routledge.

Snow, C. (2002) *Reading for Understanding: Toward an R&D Program in Reading Comprehension*. Santa Monica, CA: Rand.

Wolf, M. (2007) *Proust and the Squid*. New York: HarperCollins.

For teachers interested in nurturing agency in schools, this book offers an accessible way into the concept and outlines how classrooms can become more responsive to children's agency:

Johnston, P. H. (2004) *Choice Words: How Our Language Affects Children's Learning*. Portland, ME: Stenhouse.

2
Summary of research on children's digital books

This chapter aims to provide a concise summary of the existing empirical evidence concerning children's digital books. In selecting the studies for this review, I was guided by two principal aims: to include interdisciplinary evidence that uses mixed methods in examining the relationship between digital books and children's learning, and to give equal weight to both positive and negative impacts of children's digital books. Although I tried to include studies that were conducted in various countries, I could not escape the fact that the current evidence base is dominated by Anglo-American research with a quantitative orientation.

Introduction to the research on children's digital books

The novelty of screens and the vast amount of mediocre and inappropriate content that can be accessed through them have, understandably, led to some concerns about the negative effect of screens on the coveted activity of reading. I understand and share some of the concerns. It is important that we all engage in a considered reflection on both the benefits and limitations of reading on screen.

You may want to begin the reflection with the question of novelty and the challenge of new developments that are often perceived as a threat rather than an opportunity. Although decades of research demonstrate the beneficial effects of children's reading print/paper books, research on children's use of screens still needs to develop. A major challenge faced by research on emerging technologies is that its findings are typically based on single rather than repeated studies and on short-term and small-scale rather than longitudinal and large-scale investigations. One of the key questions that researchers therefore need to ask is what are the most relevant *features* and *effects* that they should examine in a given research context. You can think of 'features' in terms of the characteristics of digital books that influence children's learning. For example, multimedia features of digital books are one variable that psychology research teams study and often break down into specific media such as, for instance, the presence of music or video images. The 'effects' are the outcomes of children's reading of digital books, that is, the learning gains or losses for a specific child or group of children.

When it comes to children's reading digital books and online texts, researchers need to answer questions around the process of reading as well as the screen on which the reading occurs. Given this book's focus on reading for pleasure, I have focused on research that investigates the relationships between digital books and children's literacy-related skills. There are, however, many other things that researchers study and that you might be interested in exploring further. For instance, digital books could be used to foster children's creativity or they could be used to support children's acquisition of factual knowledge, coding and computational thinking, fine motor skills or spatial recognition. As with any multifunctional tool, there is significant potential to support various skills (and for researchers to study the effectiveness of that support).

My focus on digital books as a specific type of children's engagement with screens is narrow but also specific to ensure a more thorough discussion of the key issues. After a résumé of research on digital books, I zoom in on personalised books and the influence of personalisation on children's learning with books. I break down the research findings in relation to their relevance for specific features of digital books and then the effects of these features.

The influence of the features of children's books on children's learning

Early experimental research on children's digital books began as comparative research in which researchers compared the effects of children's digital books against the effects of print books. For example, Segal-Drori, Korat, Shamir and Klein (2010) compared children's learning of reading-related skills with e-books and print books with and without adults' support. They found that reading the e-book with adult instruction was the most beneficial option and led to higher levels of children's learning than reading the print book alone or the print book with adult instruction. Researchers have also compared different kinds of e-books. For example, Parish-Morris, Mahajan, Hirsh-Pasek, Golinkoff and Collins (2013) compared the level of dialogue between parents and children and the children's story comprehension after they read one of three types of books: electronic console book, CD-ROM book and interactive multimedia digital book. They found that the more electronic features there were in the book, the lower the children's understanding of the story and the parent–child dialogue. The e-book/print book comparative studies indicated that so long as electronic books provide space for parents to have a conversation with their child about the story content, they may be a viable alternative to print books. However, the challenge of comparative studies is to ensure that researchers compare like with like, which is not always possible with e-books. You saw in Chapter 1 the many different types and kinds of e-books out there. A more nuanced approach is therefore to compare different *characteristics* of digital books and print books or to study digital books in their own right. In the latter case, researchers have examined the effects of multimedia and interactive features on children's learning.

Considering the influence of multimedia features in children's digital books

Multimedia features in digital books have been mostly studied in relation to the presence of audio features, that is, sounds, music and spoken narrative. These are key distinguishing characteristics of digital books: digital books are different from print books because they have words that can be highlighted when spoken aloud by the recorded voice. Some digital books display the text passage and highlight in colour the individual words that are read aloud, and some digital books display the individual words one by one as they are being spoken aloud. This feature is an important teaching technique for children's word recognition and letter knowledge, especially for children who struggle with recognising letters on the page. So much so that an early study by the Dutch researchers de Jong and Bus (2002) examining this feature in simple e-books found that digitally spoken text accompanied with corresponding written text that was highlighted as it was being spoken was for some children a more effective teaching tool than an adult reading from a print book with the child. The authors suggested that this might be because the digital format is more attractive to children in that the spoken words get highlighted in colour as soon as children tap the icon whereas words in print books are static and lack any special visual effects. De Jong and Bus concluded that 'Exploration of electronic books is not a replacement for regular book-reading sessions but a valuable supplement' (p. 154).

A key aspect of investigation by researchers has been whether the audio features of digital books are related to the storyline or not and how this alignment may influence children's understanding of the story. This focus of research is important because there is a great variety in the current design of children's popular digital books: some digital books contain music that interferes with the voiceover or distracts the child from the text, and some digital books have music to enhance the story plot. For example, in the *Little Red Riding Hood* digital book by Nosy Crow, there are pages that play calm background music (for example when Little Red Riding Hood is using a jar to get water from a pond) as well as simple sounds (for example when Little Red Riding Hood knocks on the door of Grandma's house). Most researchers agree that audio features aligned with the storyline support children's learning. For instance, researchers at the Bar-Ilan University found out that calming music played in the background of a digital book enhances children's story comprehension (Shabat & Korat 2017).

Considering the influence of interactive features in children's digital books

Studies that examine interactive features have focused on two main mechanisms that support children's learning from digital books: hotspots that activate words when children touch them and hotspots that animate/move the book's illustrations. Verhallen and Bus (2010) studied the latter with 92 immigrant, low-income five-year-olds living in the Netherlands, who read digital books with images that either moved or did not move. The researchers found that the children who read digital books with moving images learnt the words in the book better than children who read the same book but with static images. The researchers hypothesise that this may be because the movement helped children make an association between word and illustration. Children who are beginning to read get most of their story understanding from the illustrations, so enhancing the illustrations may facilitate the learning process. It is important to note that the illustrations in the study matched the story text and as such acted as a scaffold for the child to understand the words. This is different from digital books that include shiny illustrations and 'bells and whistles' that engage the child but do little to teach them new words. There is an appealing possibility of teaching children new words through interactive features and animated words, that is, words that get highlighted and explain the meaning when touched by the child (Smeets & Bus 2012).

The benefits of interactive features for children's language outcomes hold not only for children's first language but also if they are learning a second language. Walker, Adams, Restrepo, Fialko and Glenberg (2017) examined how children who were not native English speakers performed on different tasks of reading comprehension when the digital books they read contained additional support in Spanish. They found that adding some interactive support in children's native language improved these children's performance, since it supported their understanding of the story meaning. The added interactivity supported children's understanding of stories not only in Spanish but also in English. It thus seems to be the case that if interactivity is well applied to specifically target language cues, it can support children's understanding of a story, even if this story appears in a language they are not proficient in.

Considering the outcomes and effects of children's reading on screen

The studies I have described so far were conducted in university laboratories and used digital books designed or co-designed by the researchers for the purpose of studying specific features of the books. The content and features of the books were therefore controlled and carefully crafted. Yet, the quality of the digital books that children actually interact with – and that their parents can buy from the App Stores – is far from the quality of researcher-developed digital books. The reasons for this are multiple (e.g. it takes time to translate research findings into products and not all findings make it to designers anyway) but suffice it to say that this is an issue that researchers and designers need to be actively working on.

Rather than testing specific features of digital books and what might work in a structured environment, researchers with an ethnographic, post-humanist or qualitative orientation apply other methods and ask other questions. Experimental studies compare and contrast one book feature against another one, while keeping all other variables under control. Such a methodology allows experimental researchers to answer precise questions and attribute specific effects to specific features. Qualitative researchers do not restrict or control the 'external variables' that influence a child's experience, but rather acknowledge the combined influence of multiple factors on children's learning. These researchers study how children interact with existing apps or digital books in their homes and classrooms, in order to document children's experiences with them in their full complexity. The different methodological approaches mean that qualitative and experimental researchers can provide different insights into the overall value of a digital book for children's learning. Whereas experimental researchers study whether digital books impact on children's learning of words or story comprehension, for example, qualitative researchers study children's general engagement with digital books. For qualitative researchers, digital books are a unique context in which to document how children practise their digital literacies.

Digital literacies

'Digital literacy' is defined by Sefton-Green, Marsh, Erstad and Flewitt (2016) as 'a social practice that involves reading, writing and multimodal meaning-making through the use of a range of digital technologies. It describes literacy events and practices that involve digital technologies, but which may also involve non-digital practices. Digital literacy can cross online/offline and material/immaterial boundaries and, as a consequence, create complex communication trajectories across time and space (Leander and Sheehy 2004; Burnett 2014). Using "reading" and "writing" in their broadest terms, digital literacy can involve accessing, using and analysing texts in addition to their production and dissemination' (p. 15).

One of the researchers interested in children's digital literacy and multimedia books, Karen Wohlwend from Indiana University, has been studying children's interactions with iPads in relation to collaborative composing. Wohlwend has richly documented the many ways in which children can compose their own story worlds with story-related apps. She has explored children's collaborative composing using iPads and noted the generative opportunities the medium provides for children to author their own texts, as well as the range of different touch moves children need to perform to understand digital narratives (Wohlwend 2015). She describes how children browse, click, tap, drag, navigate and otherwise interact with a digital story, providing insights into children's active role when interacting with hotspots in a digital book. In her study of children's use of touchscreens, Wohlwend (2015) was particularly interested in the complex layering of meaning that occurs when children use digital puppetry. To make their digital puppets move, children need to decide on the story characters, the backdrop for the scene, sound effects and voiceover/narration for the individual puppets. They need to combine these distinct elements into a coherent narrative, acting as narrators, designers, composers and scene directors. When sharing their video-recorded narratives with their peers, children learn what makes a narrative appealing to their friends and other audiences and they can take this understanding to a revised version of their story. The multimedia features in story-making thus offer a particularly fertile ground for children to experiment with, learn and practise a range of composing and critical literacy skills. Together with other researchers in the field of digital literacies (for example Cathy Burnett and Guy Merchant at Sheffield Hallam University), Wohlwend argues that digital books and apps offer important opportunities for children to practise a range of new digital literacies.

The influence of the content of children's books on children's learning

So far, I have outlined research studies that examine specific features of digital books. These features draw connecting lines between the format of the digital book and its content. The content of a digital book therefore influences child's learning and experience too.

Content quality in the case of a digital story relates to the quality of its text and illustrations. High-quality books (print or digital) typically contain strong grammatical structures and introduce children to vocabulary they may not know. Award-winning children's books feature text that is simple to read but also carries a complex story, often with several layers of meaning, so that it can be reread several times and its meaning cemented in a child's memory. High-quality books have illustrations that use zoom-in and zoom-out effects to convey emotions or characteristics of the story characters. Award-winning books also feature illustrations that complement the text with extra detail and explanation. Quality of content can also be interpreted in terms of its accessibility for children from diverse backgrounds and of the values transmitted through the narrative. All-time classics often have stories with a strong moral message, empathy and humour. These markers of quality in children's books are applicable to both print and digital books. However, whereas the content of print children's books has enjoyed a long tradition of being produced, consumed and evaluated, content development in digital books is very much in its infancy. Publishers of children's digital books face the commercial pressures of content producers in other media such as filmmakers and professional photographers. The App Stores have been described as the 'biggest shops with the smallest shopping window', which reflects the large number of products they sell and the narrow selection of products visible to the consumer. To feature in the small shop window, producers need to compete with major and well-known publishers and authors who are supported by large marketing budgets. For small publishers or indie writers, the return on investment is minimal unless they produce a bestseller and sell millions of copies. Given these wider trends, it is perhaps not surprising that when researchers have systematically investigated the quality of content in the currently most popular children's digital books the results have been disappointing. A group of European researchers (Sari et al. 2017) found that the most popular digital books in Hungary, Turkey, Greece and the Netherlands have extremely low levels of quality and often don't even offer stories in the local language. A group of US researchers (Vaala et al. 2015) found that the bestselling digital books focus on promoting basic reading-acquisition skills but do not expand children's reading creatively or imaginatively.

This concern is relevant to the education of all children, but particularly children from disadvantaged backgrounds. Unlike that of print books, technology ownership is high among all sections of the population and research shows that children from lower socio-economic backgrounds engage with mobile phone applications on a frequent basis (Kabali et al. 2015). If the quality of apps' educational content is low and if many of the children who engage with this content are ones in need of more educational stimulation, then apps are exacerbating existing inequalities in society. This is the so-called 'second app gap', pertaining to the ways in which technologies are used in rich and poor families (e.g. Vaala et al. 2015), beyond the 'first app gap' of access and availability.

To address the lack of digital books in local languages and the quality of digital content more broadly, a pan-European group funded by the COST (European Cooperation in Science and Technology) Action called DigiLitEY (Digital Literacy and Multimodal Practices in the Early Years) has issued a set of guidelines to encourage better quality in children's digital books. Given the potential of multimedia and interactive features in digital books to foster children's literacy skills, it seems important that publishers think more seriously about digital books and invest in higher-quality content. The group also suggests that developers allow content to be optimised for speakers of other languages and that in some countries direct government support may be necessary to cover translation costs. The cost shouldn't need to be high; once an app has been set up to be localised into other languages, the cost of adding another language is essentially only the cost of getting the text translated. If this cost was subsidised for smaller languages, more developers might be motivated to offer content in multiple languages.

An alternative suggestion is that the translation of content be crowdsourced and/or supplied by users, who could create their own digital books. This is the approach promoted in this textbook; Chapters 6, 7 and 8 are dedicated to strategies involving teachers, parents and children in personalising digital books and producing their own content. The next section reviews research on personalised books produced by children, parents, teachers and researchers.

Personalised books

Personalised print books

Personalised books can be both printed and digital. Research has examined the effects of both formats on children's language and reading skills as well as socio-emotional skills. In some of my early work with colleagues at the Open University, we examined how children's learning of new words changed in relation to books that were either personalised to them or non-personalised. The personalised books contained children's names, photos and favourite things they liked to do and both the personalised and non-personalised books contained some new words the children didn't know before the beginning of the study. The books were produced by us, researchers, using information and photographs provided by the children's parents. In Kucirkova, Messer and Sheehy (2014a) we found that children learnt more new words if these appeared in the personalised book. In Kucirkova, Messer and Sheehy (2014b) we found that children spoke more when reading the personalised books, that is, they spontaneously described the illustrations and told the adult reading with them about their personal experiences. This spontaneous speech during reading personalised books may have been one mechanism through which children learnt the unknown words. In another study examining printed personalised books, DeMoulin (2001) found that using rhymes together with personalisation can boost children's reading skills. In DeMoulin's and my studies, personalised books were created for the children with the help of their parents. When children could create their own personalised books, it contributed to home–school and community dialogue (Bernhard et al. 2008) and parent–child shared book reading at home (Janes & Kermani 2001), which are the two key aspects that I focus on in this book.

A limitation of personalised books is that they draw children's attention to themselves, which can result in self-centred speech around the book. In a comparison study with personalised and non-personalised books (Kucirkova 2014c), we found that children referred to themselves much more when reading personalised books, by using personal pronouns and adjectives such as 'me' and 'my'. Given that most personalised books are about a child's experience, questions may be raised about the extent to which these books can teach children about other people's emotions or experiences. A healthy balance between personalised and non-personalised books is necessary for books to both motivate children to read and show them alternative worlds and viewpoints. Even more importantly, research on personalised books powerfully drives home the message that adults' role in mediating children's reading of books is accentuated with books that deepen – and at times temper – the connections between children's personal and fictional lives.

Personalised digital books and multimedia features

Digital books contain multimedia features. Multimedia features that can be personalised in children's digital books include the use of children's own photographs (visual personalisation), children's own voiceovers (audio personalisation), children's own texts (textual personalisation) and children's own illustrations and drawings (artistic personalisation). Not all digital books allow users' own input, so personalised multimedia features are not a standard feature studied by researchers. So far, most research has focused on digital books that are personalised because they were created by the child with a story-making application.

For example, in a study with seven-year-old multilingual children in the US, Rowe (2018) showed how the opportunity to audio-record their own sounds in digital books meant that multilingual children could translate the digital books for each other, creating bilingual digital books. The study found that children enjoyed creating their own multimedia bilingual books and skilfully integrated drawings, photos and audio-recordings into their books, enriching the classroom's provision of literacy resources.

In homes and communities, digital books can be enhanced with a voiceover that is audio-recorded by a parent or carer of the child. In one of my early studies, a mother created a digital book for her daughter based on their recent holiday to Greece. The mother used the girl's Barbie as the main story character and audio-recorded an engaging voice-over pretending to be various story characters in the book. Her daughter loved the book and repeatedly requested it to be read. The observation of the session showed a lot of positive affect and bonding between the parent and child reading the personalised digital book together (Kucirkova et al. 2013).

Personalised digital books and interactive features

In children's actual use of digital books, there isn't a staunch distinction between interactivity and personalisation and there is also an overlap between interactivity and multimedia. This is why many qualitative researchers study all four aspects together. For example, Aliagas and Margallo (2017) studied children's experiences with digital books at home and focused on interactivity, which was often interwoven with multimedia effects. The researchers studied four Spanish families using digital books for two years and analysed children's experiences of interactivity with qualitative approaches such as video observations and interviews with the parents. Their study showed that interactivity is more than just children tapping on hotspots that trigger a certain sound effect. There was interactivity between the digital book and the child's response and, according to Aliagas and Margallo, it contributed to the child's sense of being part of the story. The four children studied by the researchers were particularly immersed in the story narratives when they could touch the story characters and become the story's co-authors or even one of its characters. The study provides an example of interactivity that carries the potential to transform children's experiences with stories.

In studying interactivity, it is important to first understand the various types of interactivity that digital books contain. Kiousis (2002, p. 357) noted in relation to the study of interactivity in digital games, 'A major limitation with some experimental inquiries is that a condition is often called "interactive" without considering multiple levels of the variable.' What Kiousis means by 'multiple levels' are the different kinds of interactive engagement a child can have with the screen, from miniature games that are unrelated to the story to immersive involvement when the reader takes on the persona of a story character. I had the opportunity to look at the various kinds of interactivity in a systematic manner during my advisory role with the National Literacy Trust, a UK literacy charity to develop the curated database of Literacy Apps (http://literacyapps.literacytrust.org.uk/). When developing this database, I reviewed the 100 most popular literacy-oriented apps available from the App Store and Google Play in English. According to this review, there are five different categories of interactivity in children's digital books. First, interactivity involves the use of senses, which with some innovative digital books means not only touch and sight but also taste and odour that are added to the reading experience. Second, as mentioned earlier, hotspots can be linked to words and matching illustrations to prompt explanations. Third, hotspots can be used to grab attention, such as with problem-solving features and questions or commands to the user. Fourth, the story can be enhanced by computer vision techniques such as virtual reality and augmented reality. Fifth, there are personalised interactive features that are based on datafication. Taking this broader perspective on interactivity, it is important to recognise that designers use interactivity for various purposes. In some digital books interactivity is used to highlight text and teach children new words, but it is also, or mainly, used to engage them in the story, as shown by Aliagas and Margallo (2017).

While some researchers draw strict boundaries between digital games and digital books, other researchers study their points of convergence. If we were to adopt the latter stance, we could usefully include here research that examines children's word learning from interactive digital games. Aghlara and Tamjid (2011) compared Iranian children's learning of vocabulary with a digital game and from traditional face-to-face teaching. They found that the opportunity for children to actively interact with new words as they played the game led to higher vocabulary scores than in the children in the control group. Dictionaries can potentially disrupt the story narrative but in doing so they can teach children new words, as shown in this study. The research findings lead us to the conclusion that conceptualising digital interactive books as a binary choice between a game and a printed book may preclude several generative possibilities and their additional features. The context of reading and the individual child who is reading are crucial factors in the learning outcomes.

Chapter summary

In this chapter you learnt that:

- questions around benefits and limitations of digital books can be answered through paying attention to their multimedia and interactive features;
- multimedia features of children's digital books which are aligned with the storyline can increase children's story comprehension and vocabulary learning;
- some interactive features, such as highlighting text or adding narration in the child's native language, can enhance children's story comprehension;
- personalised multimedia and interactive books provide a strong context for immersion and story enjoyment;
- digital books can foster children's digital literacy, particularly in relation to knowing how to navigate digital content;
- Research evidence needs to be interpreted with attention paid to the diverse research methods and research traditions applied to the study of children's digital books.

Further reading

Reading on screen:

Guernsey, L. & Levine, M. H. (2015) *Tap, Click, Read: Growing Readers in a World of Screens.* New York: John Wiley.

Research methods with children:

Prior, J. & Van Herwegen, J. (eds) (2016) *Practical Research with Children.* London: Routledge.

Supporting literacy more widely:

Goodwin, P. (ed.) (2017) *The Literate Classroom.* London: Routledge.

Free online articles about children's digital books:

Kucirkova, N. (2017) 'Children's reading on screen: in the beginning was the word, not a hotspot', *The Guardian,* https://www.theguardian.com/education/head-quarters/2017/dec/04/childrens-reading-on-screen-in-the-beginning-was-the-word-not-a-hotspot

Kucirkova, N. (2014) 'Shiny appy children', *The Guardian*, https://www.theguardian.com/science/head-quarters/2014/dec/15/shiny-appy-children

Kucirkova, N. (2015) 'Confused by the mysterious world of children's digital books?', *Huffington Post*, https://www.huffingtonpost.co.uk/dr-natalia-kucirkova/childrens-digital-books_b_7825836.html

Kucirkova, N. (2015) 'Personalised books: exciting but also risky times for children's stories', *Huffington Post*, https://www.huffingtonpost.co.uk/dr-natalia-kucirkova/personalised-books_b_8167436.html

Further resources

There are some fantastic online courses that provide guidance and insight concerning technology use in classrooms and the use of digital media more broadly.

Childhood in the Digital Age

This free massive open online course from the Open University and Future-Learn provides an overview of the benefits and limitations of technology use in classrooms and children's lives.
https://www.futurelearn.com/courses/childhood-in-the-digital-age

Raspberry Pi Foundation

The Raspberry Pi Foundation runs several online courses for teachers, including some face-to-face professional development training courses. The focus of the courses is mostly on coding and the benefits of open-ended hardware for computational thinking, with many ideas to inspire use of technologies in the classroom.
https://www.raspberrypi.org/training/online/

Google for Education

Google runs its own online Training Centre for educators interested in exploring technologies and their use in the classroom. This is essentially a free self-paced online course with some valuable resources (all linked to Google technologies).
https://edutrainingcenter.withgoogle.com/training

3

Children's digital books: where to find them and how to evaluate them

we do quote ⁊ this

Digital books are part of the wide range of technologies available to young children today and their use cannot be divorced from wider discussions about the presence of screens and digital media in young children's lives. I therefore begin this chapter with some thoughts on the general use of digital technologies with children and the so-called 'screen debate'. This is followed by the specific case of children's digital books. I outline criteria for choosing and evaluating digital books.

Teachers' deployment of digital books in the classroom needs to be a gradual and iterative process, which incorporates a negotiation between research and practice. Digital books involve multiple, multimodal types of engagement and their use, in many respects, revises adults' traditional notions of what it means to read and enjoy stories. To truly shift the focus from obsolete print-centric classroom practice to blended and multiple ways of reading in the digital age, teachers need to engage in reflective pedagogy. This involves a commitment to listening to children and fostering their belonging in the classroom and wider society (what I call 'reciprocity'), and an ability to make optimal choices in specific contexts (what I call 'agency'). In relation to technology, such an agentic and reciprocal pedagogy implies that teachers do not withdraw their support but rather adapt and supplement what the technology offers. In particular, they need to be aware of the key sticking points in the screen debate and to judge the quality of children's digital books. Let us look at each in turn.

The screen debate

The use of digital technologies is often referred to as the 'screen debate', which is not a very helpful designation, since the word 'screen' can be used to refer to many kinds of screens. With single-use technologies, such as cameras or dictaphones, an activity could be limited to a specific location and purpose, but with multiple-use technologies, such as tablets and smartphones, there are many dimensions that need to be considered in relation to each other. The chief characteristic of current screens is their multifunctionality, so we need multiple criteria for assessing their usefulness in our lives. I explain the criteria for assessing digital books for the purpose of reading for pleasure later in this chapter; first I want to take up the issue of 'screen time'.

For any meaningful discussion it is necessary to specify the content and format of the activity mediated by a screen: a screen can be used for reading an intriguing digital book or watching a violent YouTube video. Together with other researchers in the area of children's technology, I have advocated that the features of screens, types of activities and purpose of use be specified when one engages in the screen debate. My blog with Sonia Livingstone promotes this message and is freely available via this link:

https://theconversation.com/why-the-very-idea-of-screen-time-is-muddled-and-misguided-82347

In addition to abandoning generic (and therefore assumption-laden) terminology such as 'screen time', Professor Livingstone and I suggest that children's use of technology be evaluated in terms of the quality of their engagement. We caution against quantifying the amount of time children spend with technology, because we want to move away from the mindset that technology use is inherently wrong and for that reason its use needs to be monitored and policed. Such a mindset gives the impression that technology is somewhat separate from children's (and adults') need to communicate and relate to others via screens.

Having said that, I am by no means suggesting that there are no dangers or negative impacts from children's use of screens. Concerns expressed by organisations such as the Campaign for a Commercial-Free Childhood are worth thinking about: despite governments' actions against technology providers such as Google and its YouTube platform, there is a substantial amount of inappropriate content on the internet, which is all too easily accessible to young children. Many apps and video games are designed to hook children and they are rightly described as 'bad sugar' that needs to be not only monitored but in many cases banned. There are also significant dangers of children becoming victims of online pornography, sexualised messages and violent or extremist content.

This is why we need to be talking about screen reading

Children's online safety therefore needs to be approached with the same seriousness as their safety offline. This has been the stance and core of work of several individual advocates as well as collectives such as the UK charity the National Society for the Prevention of Cruelty to Children (NSPCC). The NSPCC was founded on the premise that child abuse is preventable and it is the responsibility of every adult to protect children from harm, in whatever shape or form it affects them. The NSPCC has grown a rich database of resources that contain advice on how to stay safe online and also runs a free helpline to answer questions relating to safe use of the internet:

https://www.nspcc.org.uk/preventing-abuse/keeping-children-safe/online-safety/

The charity provides professional development training on several safety-related topics and has become a key place where adults may seek advice on how to protect children from online abuse. If you are concerned about the safety of children's use of screens and are looking for help, practical strategies and someone to talk to, I highly recommend the advice and guidance provided by other national and local children's technology charities. For example, if your school is based in London, then the London Connected Learning Centre provides fantastic professional development training for parents, teachers and children interested in online safety:

https://londonclc.org.uk/

If you are an educator who wants to change the way in which children interact with screens and the content that is made available to them, then I invite you to consider the principles of agentic and reciprocal pedagogy, in which we all shape the 'what' and the 'how' offered to children via screens.

Adult mediation of children's use of screens

In some contexts, screens can be a rich supplement to adults' mediation, especially if they provide prompts for conversation and content expansion. However, we should not be asking the question of whether screens can replace teachers to teach topics or parents to read children goodnight stories. Rather, the question should be *how* can screens enrich adults' interactions with the children. A big caveat in the screen debate therefore is that screens should not substitute the mediating role of adults in supporting children's experiences.

[handwritten annotation: Not about replacing. current methodologies but enhancing. practice & making it more relevant]

In specifying adults' role with respect to children's screens, I shall quote from an article I co-authored with Barry Zuckerman, who is the chief of the Division of Developmental and Behavioral Pediatrics at Boston City Hospital and also a professor of pediatrics in the Department of Pediatrics and Public Health of Boston University School of Medicine. Our article outlined a guiding framework for paediatricians on the use of touchscreens by children under the age of two, which was the subject of significant debate among US and UK paediatricians and policy-makers. We concluded that

> The complex nature of potential effects of touchscreens on young children can be broken down into developmental, technology-, content- and context-related considerations. It is important to have a discussion with parents about whether touchscreens and their multipurpose use are necessary for their child to achieve certain skills and how much their child's use, let alone their own use, displaces interactions with people. For technology-related factors, the suitability of functionality and quality of each activity enabled by a specific device and specific program downloaded on this device, needs to be considered. The quality of the content and the overall suitability of the device for the child, are important. For context-related factors, the third space use of touchscreens by children under two is already occurring, but merits further evaluation. (Kucirkova & Zuckerman 2017, p. 48)

This book's focus on children's digital books is aligned with my efforts to contribute to children's educational and sensible use of screens. My aspiration is to move the screen debate forward by focusing on specific resources and activities and thereby encouraging more accurate and more effective thinking about the role of screens in children's lives. I encourage you to approach the screen debate with a willing attitude to understand a new phenomenon that needs to be regularly discussed and shaped by all members of the community – users, developers, children and adults. None of us was born with a screen in our hand; we all need to learn how to navigate them. A key learning tool is to test our assumptions by participating, designing and making. In the next chapters I will therefore try to convince you to try to use digital books with the children in your classrooms and to produce (or co-produce) your own.

Do you know why digital books are a unique form of children's reading on screen and how to tell which ones are of higher educational value? If not, read on.

The special case of children's digital books

In a report for the Cambridge Primary Review Trust, Burnett (2016) summarises the key trends in children's use of digital books and creation of their own materials. She describes the importance of children's enjoyment of reading digital books and of playing with literacy-related apps on tablets. She also highlights the growing number of children who are makers of digital content, a trend that I consider in relation to children creating their own digital books (see Chapter 6). You have seen from the previous chapter that some digital books can build exceptionally immersive worlds in which children become active agents interacting with the story characters. Almost all of the benefits of digital books are potentials that need to be exploited with the help of teachers, parents and other knowledgeable adults. When used appropriately, digital books can offer multimedia means of story engagement, including visual and audio options for the expression of ideas and feelings, which support children's motivation to read, write and share their stories.

To concretise what reading a story on screen can contribute above and beyond print books, it is useful to look in detail at a specific digital book. I shall examine the characteristics of two award-winning titles by the independent publisher Nosy Crow.

Examples of award-winning digital books

Nosy Crow's digital book *Little Red Riding Hood* is a good example of innovative approaches to traditional fairy tales and facilitating children's enjoyment of stories. In one of my studies, I observed seven mothers and their children reading together *Little Red Riding Hood* at home and noted the many opportunities it provided for children to make choices and experience a sense of belonging. The story is offered as an iPad app and can be downloaded/purchased from the App Store. Users can choose whether the app reads the story to them, that is play the audio-recorded version, or instead to use the 'read by myself' option that only presents the text and illustrations. In addition to the choice of media, users can select whether they wish to 'read only' or 'read and play', that is, read with interactive features.

There are several versions of the Little Red Riding Hood folktale. The one chosen by Nosy Crow is based on the French version 'Le Petit Chaperon Rouge'. In Nosy Crow's version, Little Red Riding Hood can choose a path when she meets the wolf in the woods. Nosy Crow's version gives the girl eight possible paths to choose from: the paths of flowers, acorns, spider, feathers, music, thistles, dandelions and bees. Each possibility leads to a different game that the girl (and the reader with her) needs to complete in order to progress to the next stage. For example, if the reader chooses the path of the thistles, Little Red Riding Hood encounters a moose who asks the girl to remove thistles from his fur. The user needs to remove the thistles one by one by dragging them away from the moose's body. In the bees option, the reader needs to pour some honey into a glass jar, which requires tilting the iPad so that no honey is spilled outside the jar. In the music option, the user needs to listen to a tune and then reproduce it with the use of three instruments (sounds) depicted on the page. The choice of the path determines not only how the girl gets to Grandma's house but also how the story ends. All story endings are the same in that the girl defeats the bad wolf, but they differ in how she defeats him. If, for example, the user chose the feathers option at the crossroads, then the story finishes with Little Red Riding Wood tickling the wolf (which he hates because he is very ticklish). This humorous take on a traditional fairy tale is enhanced through the ingenious combination of interactivity, multimedia and personalisation options. The choice of story endings on the screen allows a seamless and immersive experience of different story possibilities, which wouldn't be possible in a print version. Children can move the character around the scene and help her carry out various activities such as knocking on the door, collecting dandelions or starting to speak. The act of moving the main story characters across the digital pages enhances the feeling of being part of the story, particularly in the crossroads scene where the user makes decisions on behalf of the girl. Unlike a printed version of the fairy tale, a digital book speaks, plays music, gives readers a choice of story endings, engages them in games with the story characters and highlights the words for them as the text is spoken aloud. This digital book is thus a good example of contemporary reading experiences for children which are different from reading off screen.

The Nosy Crow app *Cinderella* has a similar design to other Nosy Crow digital books in that users can choose whether the app reads the text to them or they read it themselves and whether or not the interactive features are activated during the reading experience. Features that make the app different from a print version of 'Cinderella' include a visual Contents menu that allows users to jump to any page with a single tap.

Another difference is the interactivity of the digital book: the child can be directly involved in helping Cinderella clean the dishes or dress up her mean sisters. The digital book also has a personalisation feature: in two of the scenes, there is a mirror, which is part of the story illustration but also an opening for the iPad's front-facing camera; when the child looks into the mirror on the story page, they can see their own face. Thus the story illustration becomes personalised with the child's face, or, if they are reading with an adult, the adult's face or both the child's and adult's faces. The parallel we can draw here with print books is the use of a mirror surface at the end of board books designed for babies and toddlers. In these books, the mirror is usually the last page and is directly linked to some text that usually encourages the child to look into it, e.g. 'And who are YOU?' The difference in the digital format is that it incorporates the mirror feature in the story illustrations without breaking the continuity of the narrative. Users have the choice whether to focus on their face in the mirror.

These two examples show that digital books can give users advanced possibilities for making choices and shaping the narrative. Children's active participation in the story is encouraged by direct requests from the story characters, for example when Little Red Riding Hood says, 'Can you help me put the flowers in the basket?' or by direct self-oriented visual features such as the use of a tablet camera. These are not subtle changes to a reading experience. Children are positioned by the publisher as co-authors or co-creators of the content. They are provided with multiple access to the narrative through illustrations, text, audio-recording, music and entertaining games. While other media offer these engagement options separately and with a different level of perfection (e.g. a professionally narrated audio-book or a text-based poetic novel), digital books merge different modes of expression, potentially enhancing or cancelling out their individual influences. Researchers are only beginning to understand how these features influence children's learning.

In what follows, I detail the criteria that adults can use to evaluate digital books available for children. In discussing different criteria, we can nurture adults' as well as children's critical ability to select digital books with appropriate content. I begin with some broad general rules and then offer some rules relating to specific goals of reading. The criteria are based on best estimate judgement that combines what we know from decades of studies on children's reading in general and the latest studies on children's reading of digital books.

Criteria for selecting children's digital books

Teachers and parents often ask me to recommend specific apps or digital books for their children. I understand where their questions are coming from; in the digital Wild West, adults need some signposts and short-cuts. Towards the end of this chapter I recommend some digital books as well as sites where recommendations of children's digital books can be exchanged with peers. This chapter's aim, however, is not to provide a list of popular digital books or a recommended set of apps. Rather, I aim to promote your agency, your critical judgement and discernment when assessing the value of the content that children can access on their screens. You too can be an expert in judging children's digital books, and indeed you should position yourself as such if you want the landscape of children's books to be actively shaped by the wider community, not just by a selected few.

Related to this point is the question of recommending apps that I have co-designed or evaluated in my academic work. Given the abundance of digital content and the limited time the average parent or teacher has to mine it, a digital book with a stamp of an expert's or organisation's recommendation is likely to get selected. However, as a researcher, I feel uneasy about focusing on specific commercial products. I have declined several offers from app designers and companies asking me to 'evaluate' their specific product. I put the verb 'evaluate' in inverted commas because it is hard to imagine how a commercial partner would pay for a negative evaluation. What I prefer to do instead is to work with producers in the design and conceptualisation stages and familiarise them with patterns of children's behaviour and features of the medium which can be harnessed in a product. I always advocate discussing and co-designing new products with groups of teachers/parents and children. Such design is iterative, patient and collaborative and absolutely necessary to negotiate reciprocal trust, collaboration and a sense of belonging. On a pragmatic level, collaborative co-design is an antidote to the trial-and-error approach adopted by some companies with seemingly little regard for children's education and wellbeing. Whether you are involved in a research consultation or are evaluating existing digital books for your own use, or perhaps even designing one yourself, you may wish to reflect on the quality criteria outlined in this chapter.

Carisa Kluver's criteria

In the spirit of promoting community-led approaches to children's digital books, I begin with the criteria put forward by a former social worker, educator and mum, Carisa Kluver, who develops training for children's librarians in the US and curates the children's apps review site called Digital Storytime. Kluver lists some straightforward criteria for selecting children's digital books. She follows two sets of criteria when evaluating the physical properties of apps: criteria that are consistent across formats and criteria that are relevant to digital books. Those which are consistent across formats include:

- high-quality illustrations
- easy to read, large font
- developmentally appropriate content (length, reading level, top-ics, language)
- well written, nicely paced and chunked text
- high-quality content (not thinly disguised advertisements for games, movies, food, etc.)
- engaging content worthy of many return visits
- ways to extend activity beyond the book

Criteria specific for digital books include:

- relevant enhancements that support narrative
- seamless integration of features and enhancements
- sound effects that don't interfere with voiceover or other features
- technical polish, stability, ease of use and navigation settings, flex-ible use
- no ads, in-app purchases or links that leave the app (unless under sufficient parental gate)
- clearly identified author/illustrator/producer
- quality games or other extras (if present) that do not interrupt nar-rative or reading comprehension
  (http://digitalmediadiet.com/?p=3205&utm_content=buff-er95443&utm_medium=social&utm_source=twitter.com&utm_campaign=buffer#sthash.eKtDEWGB.dpuf)

These criteria are a practical way of gauging the current status or quality of a digital book by means of some immediately noticeable characteristics.

They can be applied to digital books that teach children reading skills or reading for enjoyment.

Criteria for supporting reading for pleasure

If the purpose of reading is reading for pleasure, then the United Kingdom Literacy Association's (UKLA's) criteria for choosing digital books may be helpful:

https://ukla.org/awards/ukla-digital-book-award

These criteria were co-developed with the literacy charity Book Trust and my former colleagues at the Open University, Teresa Cremin and Karen Littleton. The criteria are used by UK teachers who participate in the Children's Digital Best Book Award and have been used by UK teachers since 2015. The criteria focus on children's type of engagement with a digital book, which is not an immediately observable feature when you download a book: the criteria are intended to be used by teachers who see the digital books actually being used by children in the classroom. The criteria centre on the level of children's affective, creative, interactive, personalised, shared and sustained engagement in reading for pleasure.

The UKLA website has a scoring grid that describes the low- and high-level indicators for each type of engagement. The criteria are applicable not only for teachers' evaluations but also for designers to encourage more visionary development of digital books. Given the research-driven trajectory of the criteria's development and their existing use by UK teachers, I recommend you familiarise yourself with them via the UKLA site. The details are available from here:

https://ukla.org/forms/view/digital-book-award-form-evaluation-criteria

In addition to the six UKLA engagement criteria, I recommend that teachers and parents consider the blended engagement that children can experience with digital books. I outline what I mean by 'blended engagement' in more detail below.

Criteria for supporting blended engagement with children's books

A type of engagement that, as far as I know, is not currently captured in any existing evaluation framework, but is important for children's agency and reciprocity, is what I have labelled 'balanced blended engagement'. This term refers to an optimal engagement with both print and digital books or both online and offline reading. When choosing a digital book, it is important to think about whether and how it might enrich the offline versions of activities. Similarly, when using a print book, it is useful to consider its connection to digital literacies.

Most reading devices are equipped with internet access, which means that readers can potentially access big libraries of new titles. It also means that the reading experience of a story can be interrupted or extended – depending on how you look at it – with children's browsing the internet for other content or engaging in a different activity. Blended and balanced engagement is vital to ensure that children develop both traditional and new literacy skills. 'Traditional skills' here refers to knowing how to navigate a print book (such as turning pages, holding the book, noticing the spine and cover) and also general reading skills such as phoneme awareness, phonics, reading fluency and comprehension skills. 'New literacy skills' include knowing how to navigate a digital page and also skills such as focusing on digital text, composing multimedia texts, critically evaluating online information and using effective search strategies.

All these skills are necessary for today's readers, and books can support readers with their content as well as the way they are designed. In terms of content, a book could make a direct reference to online/offline activities and encourage children to engage in both virtual and actual experiences. For example, a non-fiction digital book about hedgehogs could contain activities that encourage children to search for hedgehogs in their neighbourhood as well as to search for information about hedgehogs online. In terms of design, a print book can contain a QR code that directly links the physical version to a digital version. Activities that combine children's online and offline reading can be introduced through design but also through accompanying guidance on the book's use. If designers and writers include some prompts for blended engagement, they increase the opportunities for this type of engagement to occur.

There are some digital books that already connect the virtual and physical experience of a book. For example, the print books of Nosy Crow's popular fairy tales contain a QR code that, when scanned, plays a professionally narrated audio version of the text. The use of a QR code on a print book connects the book to a digital version of the same story. There are fewer examples of digital stories encouraging children's engagement with print versions of the story. In the iBook *What Is That?*, which I authored and designed, the child is encouraged to make their own story at the end of the book with the *Our Story* app. The digital book thus encourages the child to take notice of their surroundings and involves them in taking pictures and story composition outside the digital book they have just read.

Some innovative publishers and developers have begun exploring the potential of directly connecting digital and print books in one unified reading experience. One example is the Bridging Book Project, where each page in a printed book corresponds to a digital page on the screen which has various interactive features (the printed book connects to the digital book wirelessly, through the use of magnets embedded in each of its pages). Another example are edible books created with 3D printing. With advances in olfactory technology, it is foreseeable that digital books will soon integrate various smells and scents in their design.

Criteria for supporting inclusion and diversity

Diversity in children's apps is an issue advocated for and closely studied by the Kids Inclusive and Diverse Media Action Project (KIDMAP). KIDMAP is a US-based grassroots coalition (formerly known as Diversity in Apps) of multiple stakeholders including app designers, researchers, educators and parents. The group works closely with the Joan Ganz Cooney Centre, which is an independent research and innovation lab dedicated to supporting children's meaningful interactions with digital media. Drawing on research by the Cooney Centre, the KIDMAP team has developed some very useful criteria for assessing best practice in the creation of diverse and inclusive children's media. The group's website contains a toolkit to help designers be mindful and proactive with respect to diversity not only in their products but also in the production team. The website also contains a helpful checklist that practitioners can use when evaluating digital books in relation to diversity:

https://www.joinkidmap.org/digchecklist/

Ok, Kim, Kang and Bryant (2016) developed a rubric to help practitioners evaluate apps for children with special needs. Their rubric is not specifically developed for digital books, but it contains some categories that are relevant for digital books and will be of interest to practitioners seeking to support children with special educational needs. The relevant guiding questions are:

- Motivation (Are the students engaged in learning?)
- Navigation (Is the app easy to navigate and is it easy to get help if needed?)

- Font (Is the font size adjustable/modifiable and is the font easy to read?)
- Content error and bias (Is the content free of errors and up to date?)

The authors also mention the opportunity to customise the settings and presence of visual and auditory stimuli, which fall under the category of personalisation and multimedia and have been covered by the other frameworks. The category of 'content error and bias' refers to racial or gender bias in the content of digital books and is one of the diversity considerations that need to be part of any evaluation criteria.

The criteria and your pedagogy

The evaluation criteria for children's digital books can be part of the learn–reflect–apply pedagogical cycle that I outlined in Chapter 1. So far in this textbook, you have *learnt* the key benefits and limitations of children's digital books and some criteria for evaluating their quality. This is part of your learning and competence-building. When planning a reading activity with the children in your classroom, you may find it helpful to *reflect* on the importance of the reading format in relation to specific educational goals. The reflection part is also about developing an understanding of the relationship between the format and purpose of reading. When it comes to the *application* part of the cycle, you can ensure that children do not perceive reading on screen versus reading off screen as a dichotomy but instead experience how the format and purpose of reading are connected. Such an approach will be in alignment with the blended balanced engagement criterion. When observing children using digital books you may notice that some digital books work better than others and this may be because their content is more inclusive and diverse. As you teach children, you learn new ways in which digital books enrich or constrain children's engagement, prompting your further reflection and more refined application. The pedagogical cycle is an ongoing process of agency and reciprocity, that is, your learning from others, your teaching others and your learning from others again.

The criteria for choosing digital books having been outlined, the next chapter focuses more on the 'apply' part of the pedagogical cycle and outlines some frameworks for introducing and using digital books in the classroom.

Further resources

Databases of literacy-related apps

These sites offer a curated list of reading related apps. Some apps are for practising and learning reading skills, while others offer digital books too. These sites are structured according to different children's ages, abilities and needs and are not driven by advertisements or commercial interests. I recommend using these sites when searching for relevant digital books and gauging your own understanding of 'quality'.

Common Sense Media

If you are looking for digital books that have been reviewed by professionals and scored according to a transparent framework, the Common Sense Media is a trusted review site for children's digital content, including children's digital books. To find digital books specifically, search for the category Apps under the Reviews tab and select the subject Language & Reading.
https://www.commonsensemedia.org/reviews

National Literacy Trust 'Literacy Apps'

The UK charity National Literacy Trust offers a database of expert-reviewed apps for children aged up to five years, organised according to reading engagement and learning benefit.
http://literacyapps.literacytrust.org.uk/

Moms with Apps

As the title suggests, this site features apps that have been tried, tested and rated by mothers, not teachers or academics. Moms with Apps is a popular site not only for searching for apps but also for chatting to other parents about children's use of technology.

Parent ratings of digital books are included on the site, but you need to locate them in the category of Literacy Apps.
https://momswithapps.com/

Reading Rockets list of literacy apps

Reading Rockets offers a useful overview of apps organised by topics with links to the apps' download and reviews from external websites.
http://www.readingrockets.org/literacyapps

Chapter summary

Central to the goal of promoting critical judgement among adults who facilitate children's access to digital books and a critical pedagogical approach to their use in the classroom, this chapter has discussed several criteria for selecting children's digital books. While peer and expert recommendation sites can guide teachers to specific products, awareness of criteria such as ones supporting children's reading for pleasure, diversity in content or blended engagement on and off screen can enable educators to reflect on, and contribute to, innovative and exemplary developments in the digital books reading landscape.

Reflection point

> I must judge for myself, but how can I judge, how can any man judge, unless his mind has been opened and enlarged by reading. (Adams 1961)

When I read this quote I think of the close relationship between reading and discernment. In light of this chapter, the quote reminds me that to judge a digital book and a pedagogical practice as appropriate, effective or innovative requires familiarisation with several resources and practices. The old adage that practice makes perfect is also relevant here: the more familiar you get with digital books, the more likely you will be able to discern what constitutes an appropriate resource for your classroom.

Further reading

Recommended books on children's use of technologies:

Burnett, C. & Merchant, G. (2017) 'The case of the iPad', in *The Case of the iPad*, edited by C. Burnett, G. Merchant, A. Simpson & M. Walsh, 1–14. Singapore: Springer.

Dezuanni, M., Dooley, K., Gattenhof, S. & Knight, L. (2015) *iPads in the Early Years: Developing Literacy and Creativity.* New York: Routledge.

Donohue, C. (ed.) (2014) *Technology and Digital Media in the Early Years: Tools for Teaching and Learning.* New York: Routledge.

Kucirkova, N. & Falloon, G. (eds) (2016) *Apps, Technology and Younger Learners: International Evidence for Teaching.* London: Routledge.

Kucirkova, N. & Cremin, T. (forthcoming) *Children Reading for Pleasure in the Digital Age*. London: SAGE.

Parry, B., Burnett, C. & Merchant, G. (eds) (2016) *Literacy, Media, Technology: Past, Present and Future*. London: Bloomsbury.

Sheehy, K. & Holliman, A. (eds) (2017) *Education and New Technologies: Perils and Promises for Learners*. London: Routledge.

Various research publications of the Joan Ganz Cooney Centre are freely available from the Centre's website and provide a rich insight into the variety of media use among US families:
http://joanganzcooneycenter.org/publications/

Jeremy Brueck runs a blog that teachers may be interested in following because it contains tips for using e-books in the classroom:
http://www.brueckei.org/Raised-Digital/

A useful blog is curated by postgraduate students at the Children's Literature Research Centre, Cambridge. Some of the students are involved in curating the website Literacy Apps (see Chapter 5) and occasionally publish details about the products they've reviewed.
https://cambridgechildrenslit.wordpress.com/2017/10/17/touching-art-apps-for-children-and-fine-art/

For readers interested in research studies and academic publications relating to children's reading on screen and use of digital technologies more widely, the DigiLitEY website is worth looking at:
http://digilitey.eu/publications/digilitey-publications/

A more comprehensive database of academic studies is the Database of Research compiled by the 'Ask the Mediatrician®' initiative. It focuses on multidisciplinary scientific evidence for the effects of media on children's health and development:
http://cmch.tv/parents/askthemediatrician/

4

Using digital books to support children's language and literacies

In this chapter I consider the use of existing, commercially produced, digital books in the classroom. This focus is driven by the aim to support children's communication and language skills and digital literacy. The use of digital books is connected to the school curriculum and two core subjects taught in English-speaking Western countries: English (Language and Communication) and Design Technology (Digital Literacy and Competencies). Before I outline specific strategies for implementing digital books, I explain the reasons why the teacher's role needs to be perceived as central to mediating the use of technologies in classrooms. Towards the end of the chapter, scenarios of effective practice are followed by specific examples of UK teachers using digital books in their primary school classrooms.

Teachers' role in mediating technology use in the classroom

It is worth repeating that teachers are key stakeholders in mediating access to and ways of using learning resources, including digital books. Teachers' volition, however, is not exempt from external factors. In some schools teachers have more autonomy than in others, but it would be erroneous to assume that what happens in a classroom is entirely a teacher's agenda. In relation to technology, a school's practices depend on the national policy on children's use of technology, the age group catered for and teachers' own attitudes towards technology use. Some countries are more proactive than others in introducing digital literacy skills to schools and to teacher training. For example, the Finnish government introduced digitalisation as a special investment area in 2015 (see Garbe et al. 2016) and continues to pioneer the use of technologies in state schools. In the UK and US, technology provision is more decentralised, with schools increasingly managing their own budgets independently.

Some teachers may think that their mediating role with digital books is limited because of the lack of technology in their classrooms. However, as the many examples in this book demonstrate, digital books do not need to be accessed via expensive touchscreens; they can also be introduced to the classroom on an interactive whiteboard or desktop PCs, which are present in most UK classrooms.

Teachers' own attitudes towards exploring digital texts are crucial but are not independent of the school curriculum. In *E-literature for Children: Enhancing Digital Literacy Learning*, Len Unsworth explains that children's opportunities to read on screen (or 'e-reading') very much depend on a successful marriage between teachers' facilitation and the school curriculum: 'if literary experience is to be widely nurtured in the cyberspace lives of future generations, knowledge about, and engagement with, the digital techniques of e-literature needs to be taken into account in English and literacy teaching in school contexts' (Unsworth 2006, p. 114).

In most countries, the educational curriculum is closely linked to the national government strategy and is often revised when a new party gets elected. As a result, there is often a pendulum effect in curriculum content, in that the ruling party pushes forward ideas that may clash with its opponents. For teachers who hold liberalist views of education, it is often difficult to follow a curriculum designed by conservative government advisors, and vice versa. The topics of creativity, digital literacy, community involvement and personalisation are currently sidelined in most national curricula. The efforts of teachers who are opposed to the idea of standardised tests, the schoolification of childhood and print-oriented reading practices are significantly restricted. These teachers need either to creatively interpret a restricting curriculum or find time for alternative activities in the small time margins that are available to them. This is not easy given the accountability pressure from the government and municipality representatives (as well as the children's parents). The intersection of technology and education is particularly conducive to critical reflection on these tensions. However, the full answer to curricular reforms is not a revolution in digital or media literacy. The fact that teachers have to negotiate their professional and personal agency in a busy classroom of 20-plus children needs to be considered from broader historical and international perspectives. This textbook can offer only a small glimpse into curriculum discussions relating to educational technologies and digital stories.

As it stands, the English national curriculum provides sparse reference to children's reading on screen. Nevertheless, teachers interested in introducing digital books into classrooms can find a persuasive rationale in other sources. For instance, the National Foundation for Educational Research, which is the UK's largest independent provider of research, assessment and information services for education, training and children's services, provides a freely accessible FutureLab report that comprehensively summarises the importance of children's digital participation and digital literacy: https://www.nfer.ac.uk/publications/FUTL08/FUTL08.pdf

In this report, Hague and Williamson (2009) position digital literacy in relation to digital participation in society and propose a model of processes that students engage in when demonstrating digital literacy. They suggest that digital literacy is a combination of: 'Knowledge of digital tools: hardware/software' but also 'critical skills: evaluation and contextualisation' and 'social awareness: understanding your identity, collaborating, and communicating to audiences in context' (p. 8).

Thus, advanced digital literacy skills go beyond the use of a digital book and encompass critical engagement with the text, identifying its key themes in terms of diversity and global issues and contextualising its main messages. To develop these skills, digital books need to be used in conjunction with pedagogical guidance. Some believe the pedagogical guidance can be embedded in the resources children use. Whether the guidance is inside the resource or happens around its use, the use of digital books in a classroom needs to be coordinated by skilful teachers.

The premise that teachers can and should encourage children's love of reading with all story media is shared among growing numbers of teachers. It was neatly summarised by John Murphy, an English and history teacher in Ireland: 'Introduce students to a wide variety of texts, mediums and genres – they may surprise themselves once they have faced preconceived ideas about what they consider enjoyable and embrace a diversity in what they read. Comics, ebooks, short stories, online articles and magazines shouldn't be ignored' (quoted in Williams 2014).

I focus on digital books as a means of encouraging teachers to enrich their existing practice and adopt a holistic approach to children's literacies in their classrooms. The current curriculum in Western countries is dominated by print books and print-based reading and writing skills. Given the amount of reading and writing that happens on screen in adult life, a print-centric focus doesn't seem to square with the skills that children will need when they grow up. Many researchers have been advocating a change in school curricula and promoting a curriculum more oriented towards 'meaning-making and literate practice as multimodal, multimedia and multi-sensory' (Sefton-Green et al. 2016, p. 13). Digital books can be perceived to be part of this advocated change, providing rich opportunities for multimedia and multisensory engagement. Their use in the classroom doesn't mean abandoning existing best practice. On the contrary, it is important that teachers make digital books matter by means of a teaching model that does not privilege form but does elicit active engagement with stories.

Models for introducing digital books into the classroom

There exist many teaching models that can be adapted to inspire teachers interested in using digital books. One possible pedagogy is Salmon's (2011) Five Stage Model of teaching and learning. This is not a model that will work in every context and every school, but awareness of the individual stages may inspire teachers' planning. Salmon outlines four key processes that contribute to effective education. I chose four elements that are relevant to the pedagogy of digital books. These include:

1. Planning and the importance of a clear aim.
2. Encouraging exploration and building in motivation.
3. Focus on sharing and collaboration.
4. Ensuring that learning outcomes are aligned with assessment.

I have found these four stages relevant in my observations of effective practice among the teachers I have worked with. When applied to different learning objectives, they can provide a useful framework for introducing digital books into the classroom.

Salmon's pedagogical model was originally developed for online learning and provides broad parameters for effective teaching. Roskos,

Burstein and You (2012) offer an empirical model based on their observations of effective use of digital books in the classroom.

Roskos and colleagues observed 12 children in a US kindergarten and described in detail the different ways in which these children engaged with the digital books over an eight-week period. In this period, teachers used digital books in group reading sessions and individual sessions. Group sessions were led by the teacher, who presented the digital books on the classroom's stationary touchscreen. Individual reading sessions were initiated by the children, who accessed their digital books on iPads and iPods. Roskos and colleagues highlight the various teacher-facilitated behaviours that children engaged in with digital books. They describe several types of 'multisensory behaviours, such as looking, touching and listening' and children's verbal and non-verbal communication around the books. These behaviours are not too different from children's active engagement print books. What differed from print books was that the children in Roskos and colleagues' study also engaged in a range of interactions with the book's surface, such as poking, touching and swiping. The researchers suggest that children's engagement with digital books in the classroom is characterised by various behavioural facets. They add that teachers' awareness of these various facets may encourage their occurrence in the classroom through teachers' mediation. Table 4.1 summarises children's multisensory engagement with digital books, with specific focus on haptic engagement, as well as verbal and non-verbal communication that teachers will be familiar with from print books.

Table 4.1 Facets of behaviour and communication to look for in children's engagement with digital books

Multisensory engagement	Verbal communication	Non-verbal communication	Haptic (touch) engagement
Looking	Using language	Gesturing	Swiping
Moving the book or body	Using story-specific expressions	Making facial expressions	Dragging
Listening	Speaking in native language (if applicable)	Making noises	Circular moves
Touching	Self-talk	Body posture	Tapping

Source: adapted from Roskos et al.

Frameworks for using digital books in the classroom

The MESH Guide

A useful resource available to teachers in any country is the MESH Guide, available freely from this website:

http://www.meshguides.org/.

MESH stands for 'Mapping Educational Specialist knowHow' and offers a set of guides on various topics of classroom pedagogy. The guides can be translated with Google Translate and the site is currently used by educators from 186 countries. The guides are a community resource; educators can add their own comments and resources to the site. The key asset of MESH is that it provides evidence-based guidance, that is, all the guides have been written by educational researchers. This means that the guides are based on data and can be thought of as an 'education system to generate, quality assure and update evidence-based summaries written for educators'.

I have contributed to the database with a MESH Guide for teachers who may have never used digital books before but are interested in introducing them into their classroom. The guide provides links to some of the key publications and research to guide teachers, including a step-by-step description of the process of bringing digital books into a classroom.

The guide can be accessed via this link:

http://www.meshguides.org/guides/node/567

TPACK model

Another useful framework for teachers interested in digital books was put together by Brueck and Lenhart (2015). The authors summarise from the TPACK (technological pedagogical content knowledge) perspective what teachers need to know when using e-books. TPACK was formulated by Mishra and Koehler in 2006 and stands for three overlapping types of knowledge that teachers need to mobilise when implementing digital technology in schools: technological knowledge, pedagogical knowledge, and content.

To illustrate how this framework operates in practice, let me use the example of Nosy Crow's digital book *Little Red Riding Hood*. If we were to apply the TPACK framework with this digital book, the three components would work as follows. The teachers' *technological knowledge* is the teachers' knowledge of how touchscreens work and how this specific digital book works. This includes knowledge of how, for example, to switch the app on and off, to activate the 'read to me' or 'read by myself' feature, and to increase or lower the volume. Teachers' *pedagogical knowledge* concerns how to incorporate the digital book into the existing curriculum. For example, teachers can choose to use the book to support peer learning and collaboration among individual children; or they can focus on the use of capitals in Little Red Riding Hood's name or the use of punctuation at the end of sentences or skilled word reading (encouraging the pronunciation of unfamiliar and familiar words). Teachers' *content knowledge* involves relating the book's content to a specific subject area or skills. Teachers might decide to use the Nosy Crow app in children's peer-to-peer discussion of the storyline to support story comprehension. For instance, they might ask how the different story endings (e.g. Little Red defeating the wolf by tickling him with feathers) relate to doing things others might not like (social skills and empathy) or how the reference to bees and honey relates to science and biology.

Having considered the wider framework for deploying digital books in a classroom, I now move to some specific strategies relevant to the classroom environment.

Strategies for using digital books in the classroom

When introducing digital books into the classroom, it is important to consider the entire classroom environment and the intention, or purpose, of the activity in hand. While motivating children to read might be a broader aim, teachers might wish to pursue specific educational goals with specific groups of children. Chapters 4 and 5 offer some suggestions for supporting individual children and using digital books for different types of activities.

The next section offers some ideas for how teachers can mediate children's *effective* use of digital books in their classroom in a typical classroom setting of 20–30 children per one to two teachers. Effectiveness is typically assessed by external organisations, such as the Office for Standards in Education, Children's Services and Skills (Ofsted) in the UK. My use of the word 'effective' here is different: it comprises children's enjoyment of stories, their repeated engagement with them and their sustained interest in reading. The keyword for effective use of digital books is 'personalised'. Personalising is the process through which teachers make the book more relevant to individual children's lives and understanding. They can show the book cover on the interactive whiteboard and ask children to comment on the book's colours, pictures and typography. Do the visual cues resonate with children's aesthetic preferences? Teachers can ask about children's experiences relevant to the book's topic either by prompting reminiscing or by asking them to draw a picture or recount a story. Such *verbal personalising* is part and parcel of the effective classrom reading strategies known as 'dialogic reading'. Dialogic reading also involves introducing the book title to the children, explaining the book's main ideas, modelling questions, clarifying difficult words or passages, summarising and predicting the story plot. Whether the children read in pairs, individually or in groups, dialogic reading and personalisation should be at the forefront of teachers' minds. With this clarified, let me now summarise the practical strategies that you can use with digital books in one-to-one and group-reading set-ups.

One-to-one reading sessions with digital books

One-to-one reading sessions with digital books are possible if each child has their own device, that is, if you have access to several devices in your classroom and can rotate them in such a way that each child can have their own device for a while. Individualised access to *shared* devices can be facilitated using different log-in details for individual children or a personalised digital library system (more about these in Chapter 9). If children use shared devices, then one-to-one reading needs to be scheduled so that each child can have a turn.

Individual reading with the 'read to me' feature

Digital books offer the child a one-to-one experience with a digital reader that can read the story to the child. All that teachers need to do is to instruct the children to switch on the 'read to me' feature, which provides a voice-over of the text. The children can then engage in individual reading with the pre-recorded story read to them aloud by the digital book. In a class of 30 children it is not always practical to engage in one-to-one reading sessions. Shared book reading is therefore typically a parent–child rather than teacher–child activity. Teachers may wish to support one-to-one reading with digital books by creating quiet corners in which children can access their stories. If multiple devices are available and all the children read at once, they will need headsets to be able to enjoy the voiceover. Another practical point is the risk of distraction posed by multifunctional devices. If digital books are accessed on a touchscreen with a wifi connection, it is important that they only contain books or apps for reading and have the internet function disabled. Alternatively, teachers can load up a series of relevant digital books on each child's touchscreen and allow them to choose a title from their own digital library.

In pre-school settings, digital books can be part of the school's provision of books and their content regularly updated rather as one has to refresh the titles in a physical library. A touchscreen used for reading can be placed alongside print books in a book corner, reinforcing the message that its purpose is for reading. In primary schools, digital books can be used during dedicated reading times or as part of a typical English lesson. Alternatively, digital books can be used on special occasions and offered to children as a 'golden time' activity. In many UK classrooms 'golden time' is a lesson or part of a lesson during which teachers leave the choice of activities to the children. If digital one-to-one reading is to be successful during golden time, there need to be enough devices and headsets for all the children.

Digital books to support one-to-one reading in the classroom

Given the absence of a real adult reading the book to the child in this specific arrangement, it is particularly important that the content of digital books used in children's individual reading is suitable. Before downloading a digital book, teachers need to check its ratings and description on expert and trusted review sites such as Common Sense Media or Literacy Apps, as outlined in Chapter 3. Two of my favourite digital books for one-to-one reading are *StoryPals* and the Dr Seuss books.

Story Pals
Story Pals by Expressive Solutions LLC is a story-making app that can also be used for reading stories. The app provides 24 sample stories with 'read to me' and 'read by myself' features. The stories finish with quizzes probing children's story comprehension. Some children enjoy doing quizzes; if they do, then by all means let them have fun. Generally, I'm not a great fan of story-comprehension quizzes at the end of each story, particularly if the purpose of the reading activity is to read for pleasure. As adult readers, we know what pleasure we derive from novels that we can immerse ourselves in without having to anticipate a comprehension test at the end. Children should have the same right to reading enjoyment.

With the 'read to me' feature in *Story Pals*, the text gets highlighted while it is read aloud. In the story-creating mode, children can make their own stories using precreated illustrations that they can animate or enrich with images and text. Readers can also add their own audio-recording to the story. The app will be of particular interest to children with special requirements, thanks to its multiple possibilities for adjustment; for example, it allows the enlargement or justification of text, which can be helpful for children with reading or sight difficulties.

https://itunes.apple.com/gb/app/storypals-basic/id568193934?mt=8

Dr Seuss digital books

Dr Seuss (less widely known under the author's legal name Theodor Geisel) is one of the biggest-selling authors of all time and his books are loved by children across the globe. HarperCollins Publishing converted some titles by Dr Seuss into a suite of digital books. These can be read on any reading device and accessed from the HarperCollins website. For one-to-one reading sessions I recommend activating the 'read to me' feature. The digital version preserves the unique combination of entertainment and life's precious lessons which typifies Dr Seuss's titles.

http://books.harpercollins.co.uk/dr-seuss/

One-to-one reading sessions *with* teachers' mediation

If a teacher is available to engage in a shared reading session with the child, then the benefits of adults' mediation can be had. Although a 'read to me' feature can provide an audio version of text, it cannot tailor questions and provide prompts relevant to each individual child. Adults are uniquely able to personalise the story content to a child's life, by relating the story characters or motifs to the child's own experiences and memories. This verbal personalisation of story content is extremely important for children's story comprehension and learning from stories.

Therefore, if teachers can engage in shared reading of digital books in the classroom, it is best to read them without the pre-recorded voice-over, or to supplement it with their own questions, prompts and explanations. Some digital books provide some basic story-related prompts as part of the story recording. For instance, the series iRead with Caillou by Tribal Nova were designed in collaboration with researchers at McGill University and have some suggested prompts for adults. These prompts are embedded in the digital books. The series can be purchased from the App Store and downloaded on Apple devices:

https://itunes.apple.com/us/app-bundle/iread-with-caillou-interactive-stories/id917756027?mt=8

The lead professor behind the industry–university collaboration on these Tribal Nova digital books, Susan Rvachew, runs an informative blog about children's reading on screen. On this blog she explains why and how reading digital books is different from reading print books with young children and cautions against treating digital books the same as print books when it comes to reading interactions. She suggests that parents need time to develop their own effective strategies to co-read digital books. Similar conclusions could be applied to teachers interested in co-reading digital books with children in their classrooms. It takes practice and time to find the most suitable reading strategy and it is possible that the adult–child dynamics will be different with the digital medium than what adults are used to from reading print books. When you read the digital book with a child for the first time, be patient and explore their responses. Over repeated readings, you will find your own way of accommodating the child's responses using the book's interactivity.

https://digitalmediaprojectforchildren.wordpress.com/

Group reading with digital books

Buddy reading

Children reading together, often referred to as 'buddy reading' or 'paired reading', is a popular way of involving young children in reading at school. The term 'paired reading' is sometimes used to refer to adult–child reading, but here I use it to refer to child-with-child reading. Buddy reading in the classroom has different dynamics from paired reading between adults and children. In addition to reading skills, buddy reading allows children to practise social skills such as listening, respect and mutual encouragement and also practical skills such as turn-taking and exploration of the digital page.

Buddy reading within the same class, that is with children of the same age, typically occurs with mixed ability pairs. Teachers pair up children according to their reading levels and each pair reads the same book. In buddy reading with digital books, teachers need to be aware of different levels of digital literacy among children when pairing up children. A child may be a strong reader but less familiar with a tablet, whereas another child may be proficient at digital storytelling but not at reading whole sentences. You can have each child in the pair read a different book, according to their level and preferences. The reading of text is typically led by the more advanced reader, who helps his/her reading buddy with difficult words. Teachers and teaching assistants offer help to pairs who struggle with specific words or can't agree on a shared strategy to read the book. In some schools paired reading has grown into community reading programmes in which one school sends older children to read with younger children, or adult volunteers visit the school to read with the children. Thus far, the focus of paired reading has been on print books but many schools have begun exploring buddy reading with digital books.

Christ, Wang and Erdemir (2018) have introduced buddy reading with digital books to primary schools in the US, Turkey, Greece and, most recently, Malta. The researchers report that the children engaged in a collaborative rather than tutor–tutee style of interaction when reading digital books together in pairs. They noted that in some pairs the children focused more on the interactive features in the book ('hotspot-centric reading style'), whereas other pairs focused on the text. The researchers suggest that an integrated approach, which combines text- and hotspot-focused interaction, is the most effective. According to this research, teachers may wish to steer children in a specific direction if they aim to support children's integrated reading of digital books. For instance, they can encourage children to explore the hotspots if they notice that children are not interacting with the story characters. For example, the teacher could ask the children, 'Have you tried knocking on Grandma's door? What happens if Little Red Riding Hood knocks on the door?' Similarly, teachers can encourage more text-focused behaviour if they notice that children are mainly tapping hotspots and listening to, rather than reading, the story. For instance, the teacher could suggest, 'Now it's Mario's turn to read. Jack, listen carefully to see if Mario can read the next page.'

Large-group reading

The classroom environment is uniquely positioned for group-based reading led by the teacher and focused on one book title. This form of reading engagement is in alignment with strong socio-cultural theories of early childhood education which emphasise the importance of dialogue in making meaning from texts. With print books, however, the format of the book is an essential ingredient of group reading sessions: print books have a rich tradition of so-called 'big books', which can be usefully shared with a circle of young readers. In contrast, many current digital books (such as iPad and Google Chrome ones) are designed for individual or small-group reading and are therefore less suited to large-group reading sessions.

Researchers are curious to find out how dialogue-based group reading with digital books might unfold. A research project that explores the utility of such an approach is currently being conducted in Norwegian kindergartens, led by the University of Stavanger. For teachers interested in following the Norwegian model, regular updates on the project are available from the Stavanger University website. (If you don't read Norwegian, you can open up the website in the Google Chrome web-browser, click on the 'translate' feature and Google will automatically translate the page for you.)

http://lesesenteret.uis.no/

Small-group reading

Small-group reading is often perceived as a midway house between individual and whole-classroom reading arrangements. Small-group reading is a useful strategy to prepare children for paired reading by teaching them the rules of listening, expressing meaning or taking turns in tapping the screen. Teachers are best positioned to make decisions about the size of a reading group, the book title and the grouping of children. A typical arrangement with print books is mixed-ability groups of five children, with frequent opportunities for all children to share views and ask questions. A similar arrangement can be pursued with digital books. The key difference with digital books is the size of the display screen: while print books come in various sizes and shapes, the screen is the same for all digital books. A maximum of four children will work for a group with a digital book. Teachers who use digital books for small-group reading sessions often change the positioning of the book and adjust the seating arrangements to allow all the children to access the book. For example, placing the iPad in the middle of a table and sitting around the table on small chairs may be more suitable than holding the book up to avoid screen glare. A digital book placed on a sturdy surface also makes it easier for children as well as the teacher to interact with the hotspots.

Whatever the spatial arrangement and group set-up, teachers need to be clear about the skills and knowledge they want to foster with digital books. Here are a few points to help teachers craft their rationale.

Examples from UK teachers

I outline two examples, which focus on two digital books, both of which were selected by a group of UK teachers as the best digital books produced in 2015 (the books were awarded the UKLA Digital Book Award). These two examples are described in full detail by Walker, Kucirkova and Gould (2016).

Example 1: Flip Flap Safari

Flip Flap Safari is a digital book developed by Nosy Crow and available to download for iPads only, from the App Store:

https://itunes.apple.com/gb/app/axel-schefflers-flip-flap/id897563148?mt=8

This digital book doesn't follow a narrative but it can be linked to several stories read in the classroom and can be used as part of guided reading sessions, group reading sessions or one-to-one reading experiences. Here, the 'read to me' feature is especially helpful. Interactive features of the book enable the children to create several imaginary animals. For example, they can combine a zebra with a tiger and create a 'ziger'. There are up to 121 combinations of funny animals' names and noises. The Flip Flap series is a well-known set of books by Axel Scheffler, including *Flip Flap Dogs*, *Pets*, *Farm*, *Ocean* and *Jungle*. The app is advertised for pre-schoolers but can be effectively used in primary schools, as attested by UKLA teachers. The fun part is decoding the words and finding new names for the animals. In doing this, children practise letters, phonological awareness and word meanings in an interactive and enjoyable way. *Flip Flap Safari* lends itself to small- and large-group reading sessions and can be usefully integrated into the English curriculum.

Example 2: Dino Tales

Kuato Games' *Dino Tales* is available for download from Google Play for all Android devices:

https://play.google.com/store/apps/details?id=com.kuatostu-dios.dinolife1&hl=en

as well as from Apple's App Store:

https://itunes.apple.com/gb/app/dino-tales-literacy-skills-from-creative-play/id923963949?mt=8

A unique feature of this digital book is that it contains the so-called 'tale-making engine' developed by Kuato Games. This engine runs in the background while children engage with the app, and can generate a customised version of the book for each child. As the users progress through the fictional world of their favourite dinosaur, the app registers their activity and at the end of the adventure generates a digital story based on the places the children visited with their dinosaur. Such an experience can be used in the classroom to discuss story-sequencing and story comprehension but also digital skills such as coding, data use and algorithms. Although the technology embedded in the app is complex, discussion of its impact on the child can be broken down into the key elements used by the app to customise the narrative (e.g. story characters, story locations and story paths). This activity can be used not only for reading and story-making but also story-writing and text composition. This digital book is particularly suitable for one-to-one reading sessions and golden time reading activities.

Swapping digital books and peer recommendations

As adult readers, we get books recommended by friends or by commercial sites such as Amazon ('If you bought this book you might also like … ' or 'Other people interested in this book also bought … '). As parents, we follow peer recommendations to download digital books for our children, and teachers similarly recommend titles to each other. Peer recommendations are one of the most powerful predictors of readers' choice of another title. For children, peer recommendations are equally powerful. You can encourage in your classroom a culture of peer recommendations of digital books in two ways: you can actively solicit children's tips by asking them directly to name a digital book they like and to share it with the class. Many teachers do this already with print books, not only to validate children's reading outside the classroom but also to find out children's interests. Another way of encouraging peer recommendations is to ask children to swap books among each other. This can happen in a very structured way if you ask them to rotate the digital books they have read or swap them with their partner. It can also happen in a less structured way with older children, who can directly send each other digital books via digital library systems (see more about digital libraries and how your school could subscribe to one in Chapter 9).

Supporting language and literacy skills with digital books

Children enjoy reading digital books because they grant them multiple entry points into a story. Children who are beginning to read, children who have language difficulties or children who speak a language different from the language of instruction, can access digital stories through spoken text, pictures or interactive characters. Children who can't read can listen to the story and see how it unfolds. This is enabled with the 'read to me' feature, but some stories also include help features such as explaining a difficult word when it's tapped or extra hints and tips provided by the onscreen character when children can't progress from one page to another. These features provide immediate and targeted help and also introduce children to the conventions of reading on screen.

Knowing how to access the built-in help features in digital books can be beneficial not only for children's immediate reading but also for their later independent study or reading of more complex texts. Different layers of digital texts relate not only to language support but also to language exploration and interaction. For instance, members of the Pottermore Book Club can enter an interactive forum where they can discuss their favourite parts of Harry Potter stories. In such interactions, reading and writing are visibly intertwined and children's communication skills are directly applied and refined in the interaction. Reading on screen thus provides a unique stage on which children can form, formalise and play out their reader and writer identities. Teachers who introduce digital books to their classrooms can thus introduce children to interactive story spaces.

Digital books available in the form of apps and iBooks do not allow one to add explanatory notes for individual words. However, in digital books read on Kindle desktop software, teachers can add notes to any words they think the children may find difficult. You can download the Kindle desktop software for free on any computer you have access to and display the digital books on the interactive whiteboard. Hundreds of titles are available for children's reading in the Kindle Store. Bear in mind that Kindle digital books contain text and illustrations but rarely any other media or interactive features. To support children's language and literacy skills, you can point them to specific sections of the book by adding bookmarks and also use the automatic word definitions provided by Kindle. Children will then be able to access these annotated versions on their own digital books (provided you have synched your account with theirs). Another advantage of Kindle digital books is that they can be displayed in different background colours and with various font sizes. This is especially useful for children with specific visual processing disorders, such as dyslexia or visual stress.

Supporting digital literacies

As alluded to in Chapter 2, digital literacies are differently defined by different groups of researchers, but, broadly speaking, they include: 'the creation of images, audio files, movies, gaming, and a host of other activities. They also include reading a PDF on a smartphone or reading a website from a personal tablet. Finally, they include a host of other activities and ways of using digital technologies that are in the nascent stages or will soon be created' (Massey, in Heafner 2014, p. 69). According to this definition, knowing how to read a digital book is in itself a digital literacy skill. Knowing how to create one's own version of a digital book is another important digital literacy skill, which Chapter 6 discusses in detail. It follows that supporting digital literacies is more than handing over a digital book for the child's independent use. It involves teachers' active mediation of the interaction and this mediation needs to be informed by existing best practice and innovative approaches. Teachers too need to be digitally literate. It is beyond the scope of this small textbook to outline the range of digital literacy skills that today's teachers need to develop in parallel with the children they teach. In the spirit of agency and reciprocity, it is clear that digital literacy skills cannot be imposed on teachers but can instead be crowdsourced and discussed in a community of digital users. As for the specific digital literacy skills connected to digital books, insightful advice and recommendations on effective pedagogic strategies with digital books are available from various teacher-oriented websites. Some of these websites are curated by teachers and some are set up by publishers who work in collaboration with teachers. I include a selection below.

Tips and ideas for using digital books to support digital literacies

Scholastic
Scholastic and its Book Club are very popular in the US and offer a range of free lesson plans and tips that teachers can explore for inspiration:
https://www.scholastic.com/teachers/lessons-and-ideas/

Teacher Toolkit
Practical teaching strategies and teachers' own experiences of using digital books are available on individual teachers' blogs. For example,

Teacher Toolkit is a website run by an award-winning headteacher and his blog contains freely downloadable resources on a range of topics:
https://www.teachertoolkit.co.uk/resources/

ETEC 510
ETEC 510 is a wiki page curated by students of the Design of Technology-Supported Learning Environments Course (ETEC 510) run by the University of British Columbia. The students on this course are aspiring teachers. The site offers a rich compilation of materials relevant to matters of digital literacy and digital books.
http://etec.ctlt.ubc.ca/510wiki/Main_Page

UCL Digital Education team blog
This blog, as its authors indicate, 'provides updates on institutional developments, projects we're involved in, updates on educational technology, events, case studies and personal experiences (or views!)'. You will find some thought-provoking posts by teacher educators, including musings on digital literacy, which may resonate with your own pedagogy and can be converted into teaching ideas.
http://blogs.ucl.ac.uk/digital-education/

Reading for Pleasure Open University
This website is run by the Open University in the UK and is focused on reading for pleasure with any books, print or digital. A key asset of the website are teachers' own contributions of effective practices and classroom examples. There is a section dedicated to digital books and reading on screen. If you are based in the UK and wish to share your experiences with digital books, this website may be a suitable platform.
https://researchrichpedagogies.org/research/reading-for-pleasure

In conclusion, it is worth highlighting that digital books that do not lend themselves to curriculum activities can be included in free choice activities. Remember the importance of playful learning and fostering children's wonder and delight in the classroom, as the researchers on Project Zero at Harvard University have proved (http://www.pz.harvard.edu/). For example, digital books that support the exploration of a digital narrative with several game elements may not be immediately about decoding text and making meaning of stories, but they may encourage children's motivation and participation in a reading activity. If children are to be able to make their own digital books and make discerned choices about others' digital stories, then they need opportunities to develop their agency. I therefore encourage you to think of digital books as a means to foster children's enjoyment of stories, build up their confidence and empowerment in the classroom and, through this process, engage in reading for pleasure.

Chapter summary

According to the classroom context, technical possibilities and the children's response, teachers have to decide how they will introduce digital books into the classroom. Digital books can be used to support children's language and literacy skills as well as digital literacies and social skills. Digital books are appropriate for one-to-one reading with or without direct adult stimulation, as well as buddy reading and small-group reading. Digital books have been introduced into the classroom with whatever technology is available to teachers, including PCs and interactive whiteboards (e.g. Kindle desktop software) and iPads (e.g. iBooks). Regardless of how and which digital books teachers choose to use in their classrooms, the message of this chapter is to encourage teachers to make the most of digital books to gradually apprentice children into the community of readers and digital citizens.

Reflection point

I like to compare the holiday season with the way a child listens to a favorite story. The pleasure is in the familiar way the story begins, the anticipation of familiar turns it takes, the familiar moments of suspense, and the familiar climax and ending. (Fred Rogers)

When you read this quote, think about the value a digital book might have in a child's life. How might the combination of familiarity, digital screen and story impact on children's reading enjoyment? How do digital books foster children's sense of belonging in our media-saturated world? How does children's familiarity with the interactive screen foster their sense of agency?

Further reading

These two readings may be of interest to teachers who are keen to reflect on their pedagogical practice and the ways in which the online learning environment influences their pedagogy.

Salmon, G. (2002) *E-tivities: The Key to Active Online Learning*. London: Kogan Page.
Zeichner, K. and Liu, K. (2010) 'A critical analysis of reflection as a goal for teacher education', in *Handbook of Reflection and Reflective Inquiry: Mapping a Way of Knowing for Professional Reflective Inquiry*, edited by N. Lyons, 67–83. New York: Springer.

If you are interested in how story-sharing can connect young children across the world, make sure you check Project Zero's initiative Out of Eden, at the Harvard Graduate School of Education:
http://learn.outofedenwalk.com/

5
Using digital books to support individual children

One of the greatest challenges faced by teachers is to marry children's individual profiles with collective and communal identities. In Chapter 4, I emphasised the communal aspect and aligning the use of digital books with the school curriculum. In this chapter I outline several examples and strategies for using digital books to address the needs and challenges of individual children. The examples should not be interpreted as possible treatments or therapies for children with special difficulties. Rather, my tips are offered as a collection of ideas that professionals and parents may find interesting to explore further.

Rationale for introducing digital books to individual children

Each child has a unique profile and digital books can be used to accommodate and support children's various talents and preferences. In this respect, digital books align with the role played by digital technologies more broadly: to actively involve children in co-shaping the environment they inhabit and the resources they use. Designers and developers of technologies are keenly aware of this personalisation potential. Together with academics who are involved in participatory research, some industry stakeholders advocate children's active role in technology design. As David Kleeman says on his blog: 'it's critical for children to be more than abstract signposts on the "roadmap to digital well-being". If we're to make a difference, they have to be understood as the diverse, developmentally distinct individuals who inhabit the minds and consciences of the best kids media developers.'

A child-centred approach to technology use is often gauged in the terms of personalised education. Although this book is not about personalised education per se, it would be an omission not to mention the wider landscape of technology-mediated personalised education.

Technology-mediated personalised education

You can think of 'personalised education' as education that starts from the child. I focus on personalised books and personalisation that is agentic and reciprocal, but this is not how everyone approaches personalised education. Unfortunately, personalised education has become a shibboleth among educational researchers, for in many instances 'personalised education' is synonymous with technology-driven education that does place the child at the centre but removes the teacher from the equation.

Personalised education should be mediated by both teachers and technologies, or both people and resources. Personalised education has been around since time immemorial. As I review in Kucirkova (2017b), education started as personalised one-to-one tutoring but over time turned into large-group teaching and later developed into standardised education, with the aim to level the playing field for all children. There are some macro-societal reasons why, in some quarters, there is a retreat from standardised education, but the advent of personal devices that can individualise content en masse and the political interest (such as David Miliband's manifesto for personalised education in the UK in 2004) have heightened interest in personalised education in the 2010s. Personal mobile technologies allow one to adjust display settings, to store, curate and process individual programs, such as apps and iBooks, and to dataficate children's progress, and data from the latter can be used to run learning analytics and measure and monitor children's progress. Personalised education mediated by touchscreens is underway in many UK secondary and some primary schools, and, in the US, widely in K–12 (kindergarten to Grade 12) education. Given that in these approaches most learning materials are offered to children digitally, personalised education is often perceived as driven by the technology companies rather than by the teachers in the classrooms. Teachers have approached technology-driven personalised education with considerable resistance, raising concerns about technology undermining their role as educators and sidelining their professionalism. Most educational research has been concerned with documenting the tensions inherent in technocentric business solutions to public education (see, for example, Roberts-Mahoney, Means & Garrison 2016). Rather than swinging the pendulum to personalised education at the expense of standardised education, my colleagues and I have been advocating for 'personalised pluralisation' (Kucirkova & Littleton 2016). My emphasis on reciprocity, diversity and community involvement in relation to personalised books is an instantiation of the personalised pluralisation agenda.

In this book I outline how digital books can be used for technology-*mediated* personalised education driven by teachers, parents and the children themselves. Chapters 6, 7 and 8 outline how adults and children can create or co-create their own books and use them to enrich their experiences of reading. With such human- and technology-mediated personalised learning, digital books can be used to support specific outcomes, especially if they are embedded in a rich portfolio of other reading activities in the classroom.

Research studies with digital books and children with special educational needs

Researchers have been careful to ensure that technologies and digital books are not perceived as magic bullets in the education of children with complex needs. Several case studies with digital books and children with autism document how digital books can contribute to a focus on children's capabilities rather than deficits. For example, Oakley, Howitt, Garwood and Durack (2013) describe how multimedia non-fiction digital books developed with Microsoft PowerPoint improved the attitude to reading of an eight-year-old Australian child with autism. Their findings echo those of Kucirkova, Messer, Critten and Harwood (2014c), in which we noted the potential of digital books to position children as authors and to reframe their role in the classroom. Digital books on iPads and similar tablets allow these children to be active makers and contributors, thus highlighting their capabilities rather than needs. In all my studies, however, adults' mediation of children's technology use was crucial.

Throughout this book I have tried to include strategies and ideas that have been empirically evaluated by research. However, given the novelty of digital books and the need to support diverse reading experiences, such an approach could be limiting, especially when it comes to supporting individual children's needs. This chapter is therefore mainly based on my subjective recommendations, which I hope you will approach with curiosity and your own expertise regarding the needs and preferences of the children you work with.

Children's age and use of apps

Children's age is a crude, but internationally widely used, means of differentiating as well as grouping children. For digital products developed for children, age is a typical form of market segmentation. You may have noticed on the App Store that digital books are developed and sold according to different age brackets. The age groups for selling apps on the iOS (iPhone operating system) Apple Store are divided into three categories: five years and under; six to eight; and nine to eleven. Publishers thus need to decide which category to market their app under and adults downloading apps need to select from the appropriate age band.

On Google Play, the age specification is even less granular: all content marked with a 'family star' is for children aged between zero and twelve years. This is a wide age range, so teachers and parents need to be especially careful about downloading content for the youngest age group. To identify children's content, parents have to search for the 'family star' – a green star symbol. To locate children's digital books on the store, Google provides the following guidance:

1. Open the Play Store app on your device .
2. Tap Apps & Games or Movies, Music, Books.
3. Tap Movies & TV or Books.
4. At the top, tap Family. In the Books section, select Children's Books instead.
5. From here, you can also browse content by age, family categories, or popular characters.
(https://support.google.com/googleplay/answer/6209531)

Neither Apple nor Google provides age-related guidelines on appropriate digital books, so the following section provides some broad guiding principles for the use and choice of digital books according to children's age. The age groups are defined by intervals of two years, apart from the last category of eight- to twelve-year-olds. Please bear in mind the caveat that every child is different and developmental markers are approximations.

Children under the age of two

The use of technologies by infants and babies has been the subject of intense public and scholarly discussion since the appearance of TV screens in the 1940s. The arrival of touchscreens has intensified the debate given that this new technology was not tested or calibrated for babies' use and yet can be frequently seen in babies' hands.

Given that access to touchscreens has rapidly spread among all sections of the population without any empirical evidence regarding their benefits or limitations, adults with a duty of care towards young children, such as paediatricians for example, need to take precautionary steps with respect to any potential harm. A 2011 policy statement of the American Academy of Pediatrics (AAP) Council on Communications and Media reaffirmed an earlier recommendation (AAP Committee on Public Education 1999) that children under two years old should avoid all screen media. The recommendation was later revised to state that screens may be used but always monitored by an adult (AAP Council on Communications and Media 2016). It remains the case, however, that the use of interactive screens is of little if any added value to infants' development. The first two years are a very sensitive period in which the infant builds attachment to the main caregiver, learns its first words, grows rapidly and develops hand–eye coordination with real objects. Touchscreens do not add significant value to these milestones, at least not beyond the value that traditional toys and human interaction do. Moreover, the developers of apps and digital books rarely test their products with the youngest age group (given the restrictions of access to this population), which means that the products are not optimised for babies (e.g. screen brightness may be acceptable for adult eyes but not for babies' eyes).

Based on this, it is easy to deduce that digital books are not essential to development in the first two years and are unlikely to have any greater value to babies than print books. It is possible that over time, as more developers design digital books specifically for the youngest age group, this situation will change, but as things stand, the quality of digital books for babies simply can't match that of baby board books. In addition, print books can be manipulated as objects, enabling infants to explore their surface textures (fur, mirrors), weight and shapes, and they are made of non-toxic materials (many babies chew on them). The learning opportunities offered by these features is unlikely to be replaced by the multimedia and interactive features of digital books.

Two-to four-year-olds

Two- to four-year-old children are frequent users of technology, whether that means watching TV, playing Wii or playing games on the tablet. Children in this age group will enjoy digital books that keep the focus on the story and support shared adult–child reading experiences. According to the research detailed in Chapter 2, suitable digital books are those which support basic pre-school concepts and creative engagement. When choosing digital books for this age group, it is important to be aware of some commercial trends and the tactics used by some designers of digital books. Young children are a significant market force and pre-schoolers are heavily targeted by the developers and designers of literacy apps and digital books. As Calvert (2008) points out: 'although television is still the dominant venue for advertising, marketers are exploring new ways to market to children and adolescents through online media and wireless devices, often using stealth techniques whereby consumers are immersed in branded environments, frequently without knowing that they are being exposed to sophisticated marketing campaigns' (p. 212). Designers may use children's data in exchange for the time they spend playing with an app. In light of this, I recommend you beware of digital books designed to get children hooked with various rewards rather than offering them a valuable reading experience. Digital books that contain games with only one answer and a simplistic cause–effect rewarding system do not teach children any new skills (apart from how to succeed in that game).

You should also be aware of the marketing technique of in-app purchases, that is, invitations to buy extra features within a children's digital book or literacy app. Although most in-app purchases require parental approval for purchase (for example in the form of entering a passcode to authorise the credit card transaction), a child can easily learn the steps and taps necessary to unlock locked features.

Given these pervasive marketing techniques, it is important that parents and teachers carefully check the appropriateness of a digital book advertised for children, especially its commercialisation features. Researchers agree that digital books with additional purchase options are not appropriate for pre-schoolers and that it is essential that digital book developers disclose the company's data collection and sharing practices (or include an easy opt-out option). Parents can use digital books for bedtime reading and individualise the experience for their child by adding their own story recordings. They can also choose digital books with generous illustrations and make up their own stories around these images.

Two- to four-year-old children will appreciate their parents' active involvement in co-reading digital books with them.

Four- to six-year-olds

The commercial pressures with younger pre-schoolers hold with four- to six-year-olds. Adults who choose digital books for pre-school-aged children need to be wary of any commercialisation or data-handling features. The Common Sense Media review site has a section dedicated to commercialisation; the reviewers take a stricter line with the youngest age group.

Four- to six-year-old children are in the early stages of developing their reader identity and can usefully practise their emergent literacy skills with digital books. Adults can encourage children to read a digital book to them or explain how it works. Children at this stage enjoy taking ownership of their learning and positioning themselves in the role of a teacher. Story-making apps are very popular among four- to six-year-olds, since children enjoy imagining, creating, reading and sharing their own multimedia stories. Story-making apps that encourage children's creativity, self-control and sharing are particularly suitable for this age group.

Six- to eight-year-olds

Children in this age bracket can typically read on their own and may therefore enjoy digital books they can read independently. Children may engage with digital books that encourage their interest in other areas. For example, digital books that stimulate curiosity about history or geographical topics may be of particular interest to six- to eight-year-olds. Digital books that tap into children's interests are likely to provide a lot of enjoyment, as are literacy apps that allow children to interact with their friends and family. Giving children choices not only in terms of content but also in the features of individual digital books may further enhance their identity as a reader. For independent use of digital books, it is best to choose ones that contain easily recognisable vocabulary and place a limited number of words on the screen.

Eight- to twelve-year-olds

Children aged between eight and twelve years are typically ready to read chapter books and longer stories. Eight- to twelve-year-olds may enjoy illustrations and multimedia features, but to keep them engaged and entertained the choice of appropriate digital books should consider the books' content. For example, adventure books and books with mysteries, secrets and science or mathematical riddles can be especially popular in this age group.

The next section turns our attention to atypically developing children and digital books that can be used to support specific needs, reading contexts and activities.

Supporting children with complex needs or physical disabilities

A quick word on the term 'disability' in this section. Personally, I dislike referring to children as 'disabled' or 'with a disability', since I believe the word has some dehumanising connotations. However, I recognise that the term is accepted by many people and I therefore use it in this book as a keyword to signal to practitioners who use this term that this section may be relevant for them.

There is still a long way to go with disability equality in children's products, including digital books. For a yearly updated list of most attractive and effectively designed books for children with disabilities, the International Board on Books for Young People (IBBY) produces an annual catalogue of the best titles, with short reviews and categories relevant to different types of needs and disabilities. The IBBY Collection of Books for Young People with Disabilities can be accessed on IBBY's main website:

http://www.ibby.org/awards-activities/activities/ibby-collection-of-books-for-young-people-with-disabilities/?L=0

Some of the books recommended in these yearly catalogues can be accessed as simple e-books via a web browser or a special digital reader the child may have. The market for books specially written for children with complex needs is small, which means that content diversity is limited. However, the possibility of producing digital books in a relatively easy way may open new avenues to diversify the available content. Parents, teachers and caregivers can contribute content that reflects the unique lives of their children. There are some examples that may inspire them, for instance Suzanne Berton's titles.

Suzanne Berton's e-books

These are self-produced, self-published books on various topics of special needs, disability and diversity, available as Kindle e-books or iBooks. Kindle editions can be bought via Amazon and iBooks via the iPad's iBook app. My favourite titles are *Marnie Is Deaf* and *I am Able. Quite Capable.* You can read more about them on Goodreads:

https://www.goodreads.com/author/list/2986448.Suzanne_ Berton

Obi

If you want to create digital books in a specific format, then the *Obi* app may be useful. *Obi* is a free tool for Windows OS which can be used to produce free audio-books. The program was developed by the DAISY consortium, which aims to promote Digital Accessible Information Systems. Products that comply with DAISY standards can be used by people who are blind or visually impaired. Their website contains several examples of talking books and Obi can be used to create users' own versions of digital books:

http://www.daisy.org/project/obi

Supporting children with language and reading difficulties

There are hundreds of apps designed specifically to support phonics, phonemic awareness and decoding. Many of these apps are based on a skill-drill approach and a reward system that may not be appropriate for young children. Although some contain stories as part of the teaching exercise, the stories are more or less a practice ground for basic skills rather than offering children the experience of immersing themselves in a rich narrative. Given this book's focus on the latter type of reading, I limit the recommendations of specific phonic apps here. However, there are apps that can be used for various reading skills, including phonics. For example, if the teacher's aim is to support specific reading skills in the context of stories, then the *Rhyme-to-Read* app may be suitable.

Rhyme-to-Read

Rhyme-to-Read was created by learning specialists and offers a structured approach to supporting children's independent reading of selected digital books. The books are offered through the app in a sequence of gradually increasing difficulty of 'word families'. Each book teaches a specific word family and presents new words that appear in the story, so that children can see the words they have learnt as they progress through the series. Colour-coding helps with visual discrimination of similar sounds across the book titles. The app is only available for iOS devices. More information is available from the developers' website:

http://rhymetoread.com/

Reading Machine

To support children's reading of words they might not know, spelling aid apps such as the *Reading Machine* can be useful. *Reading Machine* is available for Apple devices and facilitates reading by sounding out words children may not be familiar with. The app is essentially a dictionary into which you tap a word and the app then spells it out in a clear natural voice. By splitting the screen, children can have the app open next to the digital book they are reading.

http://www.sharpcuriosity.com/readingMachine.htm

Supporting children with dyslexia

Tints

The *Tints* app is a collection of digital books that can be read with dyslexia-friendly background colours, spacing of words and letters, irregular line lengths and the Barrington Stoke font. Other features include a sliding reading ruler to indicate progress and a choice of coloured filters to increase readability. The app can be downloaded from the App Store for iPads:

https://www.barringtonstoke.co.uk/blog/2015/10/06/introducing-tints-our-dyslexia-friendly-e-reading-app/

Nessy

Nessy is a popular program for children with dyslexia as well as children whose first language is not English. This resource can be used at school and at home and provides a range of activities to encourage children's reading, writing, spelling and typing. The developers describe *Nessy* as a multisensory game and report high satisfaction levels among teachers, parents and children across the world. The resources pack offers a set of programs for practising reading skills as well as specific dyslexia-related skills. I include *Nessy* in this section not because of its focus on discrete reading skills but because of the activities accompanying the story excerpts, through which children can develop story comprehension skills. These are connected to Nessy's core program focused on phonics, blending words, spelling, phonemic awareness, decoding, mastering sight words and increasing vocabulary. The program is designed for children's individual use and you can individualise the activities according to children's baseline level and level of progression.

https://www.nessy.com/uk/product/nessy-reading-spelling/

Adjusting the display of reading devices

Children with dyslexia are likely to enjoy mainstream digital books but may need the reading display to be adjusted. This can be easily done using the customisation features of the reading device. For iPads, iPhones and other Apple devices, you can adjust the text size and screen brightness with the settings of individual apps or digital books. For iBooks, the screen display needs to be adjusted from the iBook app. iBook users can also change the font of individual titles on the virtual bookshelf.

For Android devices, you can change the screen brightness, font size and font type. Instructions are available for each reading device in the manufacturer's user manual but can be easily located online if you search by typing in the brand name of your device (including its version number) and the keyword 'screen brightness'.

Users of Kindle readers can adjust the screen brightness and use the 'nightlight' feature. For Kindle reading devices, full instructions are available from the Amazon website: https://www.amazon.co.uk/gp/help/customer/display.html?nodeId=201733330.

Although children with dyslexia are particularly vulnerable to eye discomfort from bright screens, adjusting the reading levels is important for all children and particularly so before bedtime. To avoid eye strain from bright screens, you can download the so-called 'screen dimming apps' that are available from the App Store and Google Play with various prices and functionalities.

Supporting children with a traumatic injury

There is no one book or app that could ease the pain of losing a loved one or the experience of a traumatic event. Stories can help build bridges between past and present and support the recovery process. Some of the best print children's books written for traumatised children have been designed as apps or digital books and are worth exploring. I have selected examples that do not make reference to an afterlife or religious beliefs and that I found helpful when working with refugee children as a volunteer.

KidTrauma

There are not many titles available for Android devices which offer high-quality digital content relating to the theme of loss. What there is is an abundance of 'diagnostic' apps for ascertaining the level of children's trauma and establishing whether professional help is needed. One such app is *KidTrauma*, available from Google Play. It is not a digital book but essentially a checklist with questions to help adults determine whether a child may need professional help and how to support them in relation to specific symptoms. I include it here because I came across it being used in several volunteer groups working with children with trauma.

https://play.google.com/store/apps/details?id=com.kidtrauma.mobileapp

The Goodbye Book

The Goodbye Book by Todd Parr is a beautifully written account of loss and the uncertainty that follows loss of any kind. The digital version of the book has the 'read to me' function, so children can listen to the story and read along. The original illustrations have not lost their appeal on the screen and the poetic language of the original text is fully preserved in the digital version. The book is available as an iBook available from Apple's iBooks Store for iPads, iPods and iPhones.

https://itunes.apple.com/us/book/the-goodbye-book/id975279073?mt=11

The Heart and the Bottle

The Heart and the Bottle by Oliver Jeffers is a well-known story about loss and love. The digital version can be read with an engaging voiceover by the English actress Helena Bonham Carter. The title is offered as an iBook for Apple touchscreens.

https://itunes.apple.com/gb/book/the-heart-and-the-bottle-read-aloud-by-helena-bonham-carter/id527626216?mt=11

Stones for Grandpa

Stones for Grandpa by Renee Londner is another iBook available for iOS devices from the iBooks Store. The title reveals the main theme of the book: it deals with feelings relating to a grandfather's death. The story is about a young Jewish boy who brings stones to his grandfather's grave, supported by his family and the happy memories he has of spending time with his grandpa.

https://itunes.apple.com/us/book/stones-for-grandpa/id118967 4669?mt=11

Forget Me Not

Forget Me Not by Nancy Van Laan and Stephanie Graegin is an iBook with a theme little explored in children's books: the book follows the very realistic scenario of a family who notice that Grandma is losing her memory. They learn that she is suffering from Alzheimer's disease and, after a difficult time of decision, help her transfer to an assisted living community where she has the care she needs. The digital book works on iPads and iPods and is available from this link:

https://itunes.apple.com/us/book/forget-me-not/id8173 13477?mt=11

My Pet Is Gone

The American foundation Chance's Spot has produced a PDF book for children who experience the loss of their dog or other pet. The e-book is freely available from the foundation's website and can be read on any device via a web browser.

http://www.chancesspot.org/pdfs/childrenloss/mypetisgone.pdf

Children with ADD/ADHD

Rather than recommending specific digital books for children with ADHD, it may be more useful to focus on apps that could accompany the use of digital books with these children. Apps that help with concentration include colouring and drawing apps, memory games and organisation apps. There are also apps that help with physical activity, such as *Yoga for Kids*.

https://play.google.com/store/apps/details?id=com.HomeFitness.KidsYogaTraining

There are also apps designed to help with parents' or teachers' time management and coordination of activities for children with ADHD; these can be found by searching online for 'ADHD and management'. Children with ADHD may enjoy digital books with calming background music and extra help with spelling and decoding. An example of such an app is *Endless Reader* available from Google Play.

Endless Reader

Endless Reader is part of the Endless series of apps by Originator, Inc. These digital books feature 'endless monsters' which teach children new concepts. Children are introduced to words and stories with the endless monsters sounding out and explaining individual words. The words are used in contexts of stories, word games and sentences. Note that the series contains several in-app purchase invitations.

https://play.google.com/store/apps/details?id=com.originatorkids.EndlessReader&hl=en

Supporting children with social difficulties

In Chapter 4, I outlined the option of buddy reading with digital books as a way for children to practise social skills such as shared use of a resource, shared focus on a story, and turn-taking. All good digital books can be used in this way but some story-related apps can be particularly well suited to supporting social skills in peer interactions.

The *Play Theatre* app by Nosy Crow and *Puppet Pals* by Polished Play, LLC are well suited for shared and collaborative use and have been designed with pre-school children in mind. Both apps are template based and allow children to make their own stories with a set of puppets. With *Play Theatre*, children can also add pre-recorded music and choose story characters from existing Nosy Crow fairy tales. In contrast, *Puppet Pals* allows more contemporary or realistic story characters because children can add their own cut-out puppets based on any picture they like. Thus pictures of famous actors or the children's own photos can easily become part of the story. Both apps only work on iPads. The apps enhance the visual appeal of the children's stories with a range of backdrops to choose from and several story characters that can simply be dragged on the stage. Children can record the sequence of individual puppets moving across the stage and their own voiceover for the story characters. The full story with moving and speaking puppets can be video-recorded and saved as a new digital book. When making their stories, children will practise audience awareness for multimedia content, since they need to think about the immediate and future audience of their stories. When working in pairs, children need to communicate with each other, either verbally or multimodally, as they develop the story plot and assign characteristics to the individual puppets.

Supporting children with autism

A recent research project by Remington and Fairnie (2017) found that people with autism can better detect sounds and background information when they are listening to a conversation or are engaged in another task. The study confirms that people with autism have remarkable capacity to pick up sounds from their environment, and this often distracts and overwhelms them. The researchers point out that, rather than simplifying tasks for people with autism, it may be more effective to optimally increase the perceptual load so that they can focus on a specific task, e.g. listen to music while reading. Adjusting and integrating various media into one reading experience is seamless and straightforward with digital books and can be explored with children with autism.

In my studies with Valerie Critten, a former teacher at a special needs school, we used the *Our Story* app to create, for or with children, bespoke digital books which they could later use in a flexible multimedia way. *Our Story* is freely available from the App Store for iPads and ideas for its use with various groups of children are available from the dedicated Open University webpage:

http://www.open.ac.uk/creet/main/projects/our-story

Sesame Street digital cards

The worldwide popular American television series has developed a set of narrated digital cards that can be read in a digital story format. The cards outline typical routines that all children experience, including morning/bedtime routine, brushing teeth, etc. The digital cards are designed in the form of digital pages with words, pictures and narration. They can be arranged in the form of a multimedia digital book with a choice of female, male or no narration. Children with autism may enjoy using the digital cards as they learn the importance of daily routines in their own lives.

http://autism.sesamestreet.org/daily-routine-cards/

FindMe

The *FindMe* app for iPad would be more accurately described as a game rather than a digital book, but it does contain some story elements such as pictures, text and personalisation options. *FindMe* was specifically designed for children with autism, so the illustrations, reward system and level of difficulties are adjusted to this user group. The onscreen character can be personalised with parents'/caregivers' or children's own voice. This is a feature you have to pay for and allows users to add their own voiceover to the game. It could be used to increase children's motivation and enjoyment. The app can be freely downloaded from the App Store but only works on iPad devices.

http://www.appyautism.com/en/app/findmeautism/

Social Stories

Social Stories is an Apple-compatible app developed by TouchAutism, who have created a suite of apps suitable for children with autism. This app enables the creation of simple stories or visual schedules with images and one-line text that present particular scenarios and routines and convey simple concepts. The stories can be accompanied with audio too and are very easy to make, with a brightly coloured user interface and big buttons. There is also the option of sharing the visual stories with others, which will be helpful for children who are supported by multiple adults or who simply wish to share their stories.

http://touchautism.com/app/social-stories-creator-library/

Supporting individualised assessment

In Chapter 4, I mentioned the ETEC 510 wiki page maintained by students of the University of British Columbia. The webpage features a section on digital books, titled 'Using eBooks and Online Sources to Support Literacy in the Classroom by Robert McElroy & Wanyi Wong 2014'. McElroy and Wong suggest that reading digital books with the audio-recording function could be used to remotely assess children's reading levels. This is an interesting proposition about another potential benefit of digital books: whereas with print books the teacher needs to sit next to the child, with a digital book children can audio-record their reading while sitting comfortably at home, without the pressure of the school environment.

Fonetti Ltd

The possibility of using digital books to directly record children reading is continuing to excite not only researchers but also designers and developers. For example, the digital 'listening' books developed under the Fonetti brand use a technology that can listen to the child's reading aloud (through a calibrated voice recognition system) and highlight the words that children pronounce correctly or wrongly.

https://www.fonetti.com/

Raz-Kids

Other reading systems, such as Raz-Kids, allow audio-recording by the child and then listening back by the teacher for purposes of assessment. Children can either read the story and see the highlighted text unfold in front of them, or read the story themselves and audio-record their voiceover.

https://www.raz-kids.com/

Use of apps with physical toys

Chapter 10 is dedicated to digital toys that connect to virtual story worlds; what I refer to here are physical, non-digital toys that can be used to make connections between digital and physical worlds with existing resources. This is particularly relevant to apps that connect to young children's pretend play. Toddlers often engage in pretend play with physical toys and enjoy inventing scenarios and stories about these toys. For young pre-schoolers digital books that connect toys and stories may offer innovative ways of combining the virtual and physical worlds. For example, the *Toca Tea Party* app is a great means of encouraging storytelling on and off screen. Children who enjoy playing with figures or plush toys can pretend that the tea party on the screen is a table full of delicious foods for their toys. They can incorporate in their play both their physical toys and the app's interactive design. For example, they can drag items on to the virtual table depicted on the app and position their physical toys around the screen as if they were sitting around the table.

https://tocaboca.com/app/toca-tea-party/

Reading virtually/remotely

Digital books can provide a suitable alternative to print books for shared reading at distance. This option may work particularly well for children whose parents live remotely or can't read with them in person for some reason, be this military placement, work commitments or illness. It may also be attractive to family members who do not live with the children but would like to read to them at distance, such as grandparents or uncles and aunts. Such interaction can be supported by sharing the screen via Skype to see the digital book the child is reading. This Skype option, however, is a rather static, visually limited experience.

The Kindoma *Storytime* app provides a better solution, since it allows parents and children to share a digital book synchronously. *Storytime* is essentially a library of 250 digital books that adults can read with their children over video chat with some special navigation features. The experience is similar to reading over Skype or Facetime, both readers appearing on each other's screen. In addition, there is a shared pointing feature so that each partner can see where the other partner is pointing on the digital page. This was the first app with a shared pointing feature, which the developers are expanding also for remote shared drawing. The app is available from the App Store for iPad devices:

http://kindoma.com/apps/

Another way that adults can participate in their children's reading of digital books while not being physically present is to modify the content of existing digital books for later use by the children. For example, with *Me Books* parents can audio-record their reading of the story, in their own voice and with their own story extensions, and save it in the app for their children to access later in another physical location. *Me Books* is an app with regularly updated titles for children aged between two and ten years, available from both the Apple and Google app markets:

http://madeinme.com/me-books/

Chapter summary and a note of caution

This chapter focuses on the use of digital books and literacy-related apps for individual children; it therefore suggests many possible ideas rather than unified approaches. The caveats I mentioned in the Preface are especially important for this chapter. In addition to the unmeasured effectiveness of individual resources recommended in this chapter, I wish to add a technical cautionary note on the apps, digital programs and digital books that I recommend. This may be obvious to readers who are familiar with app design, but it is worth reminding all readers that digital programs/apps need to be regularly updated in parallel with hardware updates. Whereas your iPhone or Samsung phone updates automatically, apps and programs need to be updated by their developers. This costs time and money and not all developers have the means to regularly update their products. You may therefore find that a program works well on an older device but that some functions are not supported with the latest device update. We have experienced this problem, and the financial implications of regular updates, while developing *Our Story*. Although the app was initially designed for both Android and Apple devices, over time the Android version became full of bugs and we had to remove it from the Google Play App Store. We could obtain finance to develop a new iPad version, but this, too, required regular updates because Apple was pushing out new iPad releases. If a digital book or app recommended in this book does not work as intended, please refer it to the developer, since I am not responsible for, or connected to, any of the resources listed in this book except for my earlier involvement in the design of *Our Story*. Similarly, if a webpage that I hyperlink in the book no longer responds to the link, please accept my apologies and try to locate it by searching online with the keywords in the website's name. With this caveat in mind, I hope that some of the recommended digital books and apps in this chapter will prove helpful to you.

Reflection point

> My story is the story of thousands of children from around the world. I hope it inspires others to stand up for their rights. (Malala Yousafzai)

This quote made me reflect on how individual stories relate to shared experiences. Can personal stories ever be divorced from shared stories and would children with special profiles be equally well served with stories written for mainstream children? To what extent do the digital books outlined in this chapter meet children where they are and to what extent do they expand their experiences to other children's worlds?

Further reading

Great ideas for storytelling in families with various props and story plots can be found in this classic resource for storytelling, story-making and story-sharing in child therapy. The ideas can be adapted and extended for children with diverse profiles. The book is full of step-by-step guides and examples and will inspire families and teachers alike.

Golding, K. (2014) *Using Stories to Build Bridges with Traumatized Children: Creative Ideas for Therapy, Life Story Work, Direct Work and Parenting*. London: Jessica Kingsley.

6

Children as authors of digital books

A principal focus of attention in this book so far has been on commercially produced digital books written by adults for children. This chapter turns this model on its head and discusses digital books produced by children for children. Harnessing the capacity of digital books to customise and personalise content, children can not only tailor existing content to their own preferences but can also become authors themselves. In this chapter, I take a deeper dive into story-making and story-sharing apps that allow children to create their own digital books. I outline a theoretical rationale of why children's self-made digital books can be important to their learning and wellbeing, and give practical examples of how adults can support children's digital story-making.

Why children as book authors?

The rationale for children's authorship of their own digital books rests on two contentions. One relates to the creative and empowering experience of being positioned as makers who, through reciprocity, build their own belonging in the community of writers and negotiate their understanding of stories and texts by actively participating in their creation. The other relates to the 5As of personalisation which underpin children's agency in learning. I will outline the scholarly perspective on both aspects, but first I approach the subject from a wider perspective and consider the role of children in making, personalising and using technologies.

The myth of children as digital natives

The twenty-first century is characterised by the ubiquity of digital technologies and often described as the 'digital age'. Some people attach the 'digital' label to the generation born in the 1980s (and some to the generation born circa 2000 or 2010). Some refer to children born into the world of ubiquitous technology as 'digikids', 'digital natives', 'iKids', etc. The term 'digital native', and its association with the young generation, was coined by Prensky in 2001. Prensky refers to the young generation as 'digital natives' and the older generation as 'digital immigrants' and argues that students today think and process information fundamentally differently from their predecessors, as a result of being surrounded by new technology. Although it is true that the younger generation have grown up in times characterised by screens' ubiquity and almost global internet coverage, it is not the case that all children are miraculously proficient with technologies from birth. What is true is that children are less fearful than adults and readier to experiment with new objects. The intuitive design of touchscreens makes it easy for children to explore their features and, through this exploration, to learn how the devices respond to their touch. If, however, we gave children any other intuitively designed object, say, a wooden car, they would explore it with similar curiosity, and we would not say they were native car drivers. Many researchers have therefore suggested abandoning the term 'digital natives' because it exacerbates intergenerational gaps in perceptions of technology. As Josie Fraser, a social and educational technologist, puts it: 'Phrase "digital natives" has pretty much become a shibboleth among edtech & digital inclusion communities. Using it signals the speaker doesn't really know much about technology. Or people.'

Similarly to 'digital natives', designations such as 'digital childhoods' or 'digikids' assume that children are a homogeneous group with identical capabilities and interests. In reality, families are idiosyncratic, with their own ways of being and responding to the outer world. Inspired by Steve Jobs, many people working in the technology industry raise their children with strict limitations on technology exposure at home. There are some schools that do not allow technology use at all. What binds us all is the fact that technologies are increasingly prevalent in our relationships with each other and ourselves. It is also true that, more than ever before, twenty-first-century classrooms are diverse in terms of ethnicity and gender identity. The transnational movement of families from war-torn countries, the gender equality movement and major national identity conflicts have had a great impact on today's children. I therefore suggest we celebrate children's idiosyncrasy and invite them into spaces where their individuality can come to the fore. One such space is the 'story space' and one way of encouraging children's individuality is to let children personalise it.

Children's story spaces

A story is a powerful medium by which to give coherence and meaning to an experience. The question of whether humans are wired to tell stories, or whether they tell stories because of societal traditions of portraying life as a series of stories, is a bit of a chicken-and-egg question. Stories are essential for identity development. Psychologists of early childhood, such as the wonderful Jerome Bruner, for example, assert that narrative is fundamental to constructing reality and making sense of life. In *Making Stories: Law, Literature, Life*, he writes,

> Stories reassert a kind of conventional wisdom about what can be expected, even (or especially) what can be expected to go wrong and what might be done to restore or cope with the situation. Narrative achieves these prodigies not only because of its structure per se but because of its flexibility and malleability. Not only are stories products of language, so remarkable for its sheer generativeness, permitting so many different versions to be told, but telling stories soon becomes crucial to our social interactions. How early the young child learns just the right tale for the occasion! Storytelling becomes entwined with, even at times constitutive of, cultural life. (Bruner 2003, p. 31).

Children tell stories orally but they also express them in other, non-verbal, modes. For instance, children can dance or draw their stories, or perform them as drama. Such multiple modes of sharing feelings and thoughts are important for young children, who may not know how to, or may not want to, recount their stories orally. To accommodate the range of possible story expressions available to children, I like to think of children as story-*makers* rather than storytellers. Children's story-making and making more generally, with technologies, is a very popular activity among young children.

Children as story-makers

So-called 'maker-centred learning' arose from the philosophy and efforts to position children as makers, designers and creators. Shari Tishman and Edward Clapp from Harvard University define maker-centred learning as 'a new kind of hands-on pedagogy—a responsive and flexible pedagogy that encourages community and collaboration (a do-it-together mentality), distributed teaching and learning, and crossing boundaries'. The international project MakEY (Makerspaces in the Early Years), which focuses on children's making in early years, offers several inspirational examples of children making creative and digital artefacts (see http:// makeyproject.eu/). In this textbook I focus on a specific practice of maker-centred learning: children making their own multimedia stories.

Positioning children as story-makers is a powerful mechanism to honour children's diverse experiences and those of their families and friends. A digital story can present a narrative in various ways: a story can be typed up as text, it can be performed and videoed, it can be narrated and audio-recorded, it can be based on children's drawings and photographs or it can combine various modes. Children can be story-makers with non-digital resources and indeed there is a very long tradition of children making their own games, dens and toys without electronic technology.

The idea of children making their own digital books not only builds on digital making trends but also enriches them with links to literacy and multimedia. Not all story authorship requires a new story; children can also be story editors and make changes to the text or illustrations of existing stories.

Digital story-making is very popular among four- to twelve-year-olds, who enjoy making and sharing digital games or stories with friends. A survey in 2012 by Childnet International found that a third of seven- to eleven-year-olds have created their own digital game and 12 per cent their own app (Broadbent et al. 2013). Making digital games is an aspect of the digital 'remixing' and curatorship that characterise modern arts practices. John Potter explains the novelty of digital making in *Digital Media and Learner Identity: The New Curatorship* (2012):

> Of course, appropriations, quotations, and borrowings are, and always have been, a commonplace in music, visual arts, literature, and filmmaking and in every form of cultural expression from the first stories onward. What has changed is the way in which those who have access to the digital artifacts at their fingertips have the means to take and remix content, to publish things that they have made alongside things they have created and establish new relationships between the elements to make new meanings. (p. xvi).

The pedagogy that supports children's story-making can be framed in several ways. In the context of digital stories made by children in the UK, US, Spain and Slovakia, I have been using the framework of the 5As of personalisation.

Children's story-making and the 5As of personalisation

The 5As of personalisation (Kucirkova 2017b) are a set of practical concepts for teachers who are interested in supporting children's agency and reciprocity in story-making. Agency and reciprocity are the broader scaffolding around personalisation; they provide the reasons why teachers nurture story-making with community members and give children choices and diverse materials. The 5As of personalisation are the five individual ladders inside the scaffolding which can help teachers assist children's story-making.

The 5As are not a theory but a framework that can be used to understand the importance of children's personal stories and their own involvement in producing them. The emphasis is on the content rather than the form or format of the stories. This means that the 5As apply to both digital and print books and to stories created in any genre (poetry books, comic books, novellas, simple picturebooks or multimedia narrations).

The 5As include five parameters for children's personalisation: *authorship* of their own stories, *autonomy* in producing them, *authenticity* of their contribution, *attachment* to the final product and *aesthetics* in its creation. In an article (Kucirkova 2017c), I have summarised the key ways in which the teachers I worked with used digital personal(ised) books in their classrooms. Based on my collaboration with these teachers, I developed a set of questions that can guide the activity of children's agentic story-making. The five questions are:

> To what extent are the stories based on children's own content? (Authorship)
> To what extent was the creation of the final product the child's independent work? (Autonomy)
> Who owns the final product? (Attachment)
> To what extent do children's stories capture content that is genuine and responsive to the child's own situation? (Authenticity)
> To what extent does the final product reflect the child's own taste and preference? (Aesthetics)
> (Kucirkova 2017c, p. 282)

In this chapter, I elaborate on each of these questions to illustrate the strategies teachers can adopt to support children's digital story-making in their classrooms.

Authorship. To what extent are the stories based on children's own content?

This question aims to ensure that children's story-making is not constrained by prescribed scripts for content or formats for its expression. The question directly relates to the prompts that adults may use to encourage story-making. Children's authorship of a story and adults' mediation of it need to be a tender, carefully co-constructed process. There is no official curriculum guidance on how to encourage children to share their own stories; most curricula focus on established story scripts and encourage children to recount or retell and rewrite an existing story. This approach is useful in assessing children's ability to comprehend a story, remember it and emulate a specific storytelling style. It is also used in assessing children's writing skills. The approach I wish to encourage here is different.

I would like to position children as authors who make their own stories, with their own plots and characters, of any length, shape or form. To encourage such creative authorship, adults need to make children feel that their story is in safe hands and that the seeds of their ideas are valued. Children's story-making needs to be encouraged with open-ended story prompts, calm and supportive environments and empathetic teachers who are genuinely interested in children's own stories.

Such an approach to children's authorship of stories is not unique to the making of digital stories; it applies to children's authoring of any stories, oral, written or multimedia. It aims to foster literacy and communication skills and emphasises children's curiosity, creativity and imagination. My recommended approach has many parallels with the storytelling/story-acting technique developed by Vivian Gussin Paley, which has been popularised in the UK as the Helicopter Technique by the MakeBelieve Arts Foundation and is well known in play-oriented kindergarten curricula in the US.

This technique focuses on children's personal stories that are entirely open ended, without any pre-established plot. The Helicopter Technique has only one rule for eliciting children's story-sharing: children need to tell their story to the teacher and the teacher needs to write it down as they do so. The written version of a child's story is limited to one page (a time limitation that you may wish to adopt or adapt). The child can recount any story they like and the teacher writes it down verbatim. In the case of story-making with story apps, the adult doesn't need to transcribe the story; the story-making app captures it according to the child's instructions.

The storytelling/story-acting technique has some specific instructions for the adult's role in facilitating children's authorship. According to the technique, the adult should avoid asking leading questions; they need to act as a patient listener who lets the child narrate the story for as long as it takes. Adults who support children's personal story-making should convey to the child that they are listening to them by means of their body posture, encouraging facial expression, direct eye contact and reassuring tone of voice. If they wish to support children's storytelling they can ask them to elaborate on specific details by asking specific, non-leading questions, without introducing their own ideas. The adult should not correct children's language. Children may anchor their stories in familiar tales and the adult should leave such choices up to the child. The tales that children carry in themselves may be inspired by popular stories but they do not need to follow a specific script or a sequence of beginning, middle and end. A story is whatever a child defines as a story. These specifications are best adopted in their entirety.

Authenticity. To what extent do children's stories capture content that is genuine and responsive to the child's own situation?

The way in which children's stories are solicited influences the authenticity of content. For example, if teachers prompt children to 'Tell a story about superheroes', then they prompt children's knowledge of superhero stories, including their memories of superhero stories they have read, heard or watched as well as what they know about superheroes more broadly. However, if the question is left open and the child is asked, 'Tell me a story', then the child is free to decide whether they include any heroes in their story at all.

The same principle applies to the authenticity of content generated with prompts supplied by digital technologies. If children's story-making is supported with apps and PC programs that contain templates about superheroes, then the story content is very likely to reflect these templates. Similarly, if the story-making app contains ready-made images of Cinderella, including story background and props relating to this fairy tale, then the children's creativity is constrained within a particular genre of stories.

Teachers often use worksheets in the classroom to guide children's story-making in a specific direction that is tied to a specific curriculum objective. Templates can be great to ignite imagination or prompt memory of past stories and guide children's story-making according to established standards. However, stories based on templates are not fully authentic stories. To support children's agency in story-making, children need open-ended spaces that fully invite their authorship.

Autonomy. To what extent is the creation of the final product the child's independent work?

This question is to remind teachers to nurture children's participation in active content production from a young age. The internet has increased access to existing content (through projects such as Wikipedia) as well as increasing opportunities to author content (through writing platforms such as Wordpress blogs, for example). Being a digital citizen means not only knowing where to find relevant and accurate information but also contributing information to the world wide web.

Children's autonomy in producing their own digital content will depend on their skills and abilities, which are often related to their age. Older children are more likely to produce their own written stories and self-publish them on blogs, whereas younger children may prefer picture-based digital stories. The principle of autonomy reminds teachers that children's story-making needs to be autonomous, action oriented, rather than passive consumption of stories, and independent of commercial, ideological or political pressures. Children can and should be helped to self-govern their position as producers and active receivers of stories. This is part of the democratisation potential of blogs and other open text spaces.

Autonomy in children's story-making also refers to children's discernment of appropriate tools for making and publishing their stories. Adults can support children's self-directed authorship by providing access to suitable story-making and story-sharing platforms and help them navigate the rich array of digital possibilities. I recommend several programs and apps to that end in this chapter but emphasise that, in terms of content, children's stories should be their own, personal stories which connect their own 'selves' to others.

Aesthetics. To what extent does the final product reflect the child's own taste and preference?

In many countries, children grow up surrounded by picturebooks and this experience shapes their expectations and understandings of what a story looks like and contains. You will have seen how young children try to replicate existing drawings in their own artwork, for example producing archetypical drawings of people, sun or houses with the same colours and shapes. In one of my studies with Mona Sakr (Kucirkova & Sakr 2015), we observed a father using the digital drawing tool *Tuxpaint* with his four-year-old daughter and noticed how the ready-made imagery influenced the child's creative expression. With paper and pencils there was more collaboration between her and her father, whereas with *Tuxpaint* the child enjoyed more autonomy in constructing her image. The paper-based drawing was not in alignment with the child's aesthetic expectations and she wanted to 'scribble over it', whereas she considered the digital image to correspond to adults' aesthetic expectations.

This episode is a neat illustration of the fact that children's aesthetic expression of their stories is linked to the way the story is elicited (the kind of story prompts I mentioned at the beginning of this chapter), the resources that children are provided with (the templates and features of digital books) *and* how adults interpret what children create. Adults often underestimate the different values children hold about their productions and the different meanings they associate with them. I remember a child drawing a purple sun in her story and many dots around it. When I asked her what the dots were, she said they were 'many mummies'. I would have never come up with this interpretation myself! To encourage children's authentic story-making it is important that adults listen to children. In her doctoral dissertation, Marissa McClure (2007) describes how adults who ask children to explain their drawings can learn a lot from the children's artistic interpretations. In McClure's study in a Reggio-inspired school, the teachers approached children's drawings in their own right and as an expression of the children's own worlds: 'Teachers do not "read" drawings as stand-alone. Their interpretation is neither projective nor evaluative. Rather, drawings, as a tool, help to make visible what children understand and articulate through many modes of symbolic language' (p. 117).

Children have a high sense of aesthetic understanding when it comes to their own stories, whether these are image based, audio-recorded or written by hand. In my studies with primary-school children audio-recording their stories with the *Our Story* app, I witnessed how they went through numerous drafts of the audio version of their story – a cycle of recording their voice, listening back, deleting the file and recording again, repeated five or six times per session. Teachers who support children's creation of digital stories should therefore offer adequate conditions for children to exercise their aesthetic rights.

Attachment. Who owns the final product?

Children's ownership of their final stories is linked to the ways the stories are displayed and made available for distribution. The story-making application *Our Story*, for example, allows both immediate and distant story-sharing. Users can read and play their digital book within the app in the 'use mode', in which they can swipe the digital pages and play the audio-recordings. In the 'share mode', they can share their story with other users remotely by sending it via email. There is also the option to print the story out, although of course this is only possible for the text and pictures. Each of these three sharing mechanisms carries a different potential for the child's development of attachment to their final book. Some children respond very positively to print stories and enjoy carrying them around in their pocket. They also like to share print stories with their parents, which can happen immediately when the parents pick them up from school. Other children, especially older ones, enjoy sharing their digital stories with friends and peers. For older primary-school children, the sense of belonging to a community of like-minded peers forms their long-term identity and stories are an essential vehicle on that journey.

I have explained how the 5As of personalisation can help teachers scaffold the story-making process. Frameworks are abstract conceptual tools. The rest of this chapter discusses the practical tools that teachers, parents, librarians and community workers can use to encourage children's story-making with apps.

Story sparks

The idea of children making their own digital stories is of course not my idea. You may have considered doing this with your children in the past or even created your own storybook. If you did you may have come across so-called 'story sparks'. These are little prompts, tips and starters to 'ignite' a story. There are several guides with tips for parents and teachers on how to support story-making with non-digital resources. My favourite book is *Show Me a Story* by Emily K. Neuburger (2012). This book also contains ideas for supporting children's creativity with story sparks. The story sparks are suggested story characters and places where these characters could be, as well as adjectives that could describe these characters, reasons for what happens to them, etc. Teachers may already have their own lists of story sparks if they have encouraged children's story-making in the classroom before, and many parents use everyday situations as story sparks for their children's stories (e.g. a castle becomes an obvious story spark if the family has recently visited Warwick Castle).

There are also *digital* story sparks that adults or children can use to explore their story ideas. For example, the author and creative writing teacher Bruce Van Patter has made his own 'Story Kitchen' wheel of story prompts. Children click on their selected hero, place and villain and then the tool generates a simple story the children can finish off.

http://www.brucevanpatter.com/storykitchen.html

The Oxford Owl website lists ten top tips for children writing their own stories, as well as free downloadable posters encouraging children to start a story and create their own characters. These can be accessed from the website regardless of whether your school subscribes to Oxford University Press resources:

https://www.oxfordowl.co.uk/for-home/kids-activities/how-to-write-your-best-story-ever

Bear in mind that story sparks are *a way* into children's own stories, not prescriptive templates or story scripts. If you truly want to encourage children's authentic and original stories, then you should not give them ready-made lists of characters. Children carry their own story scripts, based on the many fictional stories they have come across and their own experiences which they can fictionalise and recount. Adults are there to facilitate the journey of children's stories out to the world. In paving the way for this journey, we need to think not only of the destination but also of the purpose of children's story-making.

The purpose of children's story-making

There are many purposes and aims for facilitating children's story-making. We may think of agency and reciprocity as our overarching aims but teachers need to think also of specific purposes relating to the curriculum and to learning objectives. For teachers who wish to support children's story-making, the following questions may be helpful. Is the purpose of children's story-making

- to encourage home–school connectivity?
- to encourage children's production of books in their native language?
- to encourage children's creativity, writing and art-making?
- to enable children to express their own stories in their own way?

- to improve children's digital literacies and multimedia story-making skills?
- to provide a non-threatening space for children to practise writing and literacy skills.

Tools for children's story-making

Another practical consideration concerns the tools available to teachers and the children in their classrooms. The type of device dictates what choices of story-making apps you can use. The number of devices that children have access to dictates whether children will engage in collaborative or individual story-making. Depending what digital and human resources are available, children's digital story-making can be:

- guided by the teacher or a teaching assistant;
- guided one to one by an older child;
- collaborative story-making with peers;
- individual story-making with an app or digital story-making program.

These different scenarios are contingent upon resources, but there may also be pedagogical reasons for the support individual children need. Some children may need adult encouragement, whereas some might enjoy collaboration with their peers. As you plan your story-making session with the children in the classroom, you need to simultaneously evaluate the specifics of three key factors – the children, the resources and the purpose of the activity.

Sharing final stories

Before children start making their own stories, it is useful to have a discussion with them about the intended audience. In the school context, this discussion can be facilitated by teachers but also by authors or illustrators. There are various schemes that support the visits of published authors to classrooms (for example, Patrons of Reading in the UK) and some authors can also take part virtually by means of video-conferencing or indeed writing. When children share their self-made stories, the presence of adults important in their lives enhances their sense of pride and belonging. Teachers can reflect on this as they contemplate the various audiences and possibilities for children's self-made stories:

- the whole class (e.g. using the interactive whiteboard);
- children's parents (e.g. as printed booklets or e-books emailed to parents);
- on the screen in a one-to-one with the child's friend or teacher;
- on the screen in a small group with the child's peers;
- electronically with a remote group of children or distant family members;
- electronically or, in the case of a classroom visit, in person with a children's author or illustrator;
- orally at a classroom assembly with other children, teachers, parents and local community members;
- the story is not shared and remains the child's private personal story.

In the community context, there may be wider and more permanent ways of sharing, such as archiving children's stories on the community's website or including it in the local museum archive. Remember that if children's stories are produced digitally, it does not follow that they need to keep the digital format forever. Many story-making apps support printing out final stories or even publishing them as professional-looking paperbacks and hardbacks. Printed stories are especially popular in families (e.g. making a digital story for Grandpa) or friends (e.g. making a digital story for a friend's birthday).

Audience awareness is important not only for final stories but also for the process of story-making. If adults are interested in documenting children's story-making process, they need to discuss this with the children and ascertain whether they are happy to be filmed or photographed. In a photo-saturated culture, adults often assume that children don't mind being photographed but it is always worth discussing this with them, especially in the sensitive context of personal story-making. As a rule of thumb, always ask the child's permission before sharing their stories and inform the child about the audience for their story before the story-making begins.

Which story-making apps to use?

The choice of story-making app will depend on the digital device that children have access to. The type of technology and the specific apps/programs that come with the technology will influence the multimedia options and aesthetic appeal of the final story. There are differences in the ways different programs integrate the sound with pictures, for example, or the ways the programs generate final story files. Some story-making apps, particularly those for touchscreens, allow immediate picture-taking and picture insertion with the embedded camera, whereas others require pictures to be taken beforehand. Some programs allow children to print their stories out; some support online file-sharing. Some programs directly support children's digital drawing, whereas others don't have this option. I list in this chapter several story-making programs that I have used with children myself or observed teachers using in their classroom. Bear in mind that some apps work better than others, depending on the context of use, and my list of recommended apps is by no means exhaustive.

Examples of story-making apps and programs

NB. As with other recommended resources in this book, the order in which the individual programs appear is arbitrary.

Story Jumper and Storybird

These are a number of story-making programs developed for US teachers and international communities.

Story Jumper is free to use, but users need to pay if they want their finished stories as printed hardbacks or paperbacks or to download them as e-books or audio-books (the prices are in US dollars). This software may be more useful for US-based teachers, since the community resources offer advice specifically linked to the Common Core curriculum. *Story Jumper* works on desktop computers and has an easy-to-use interface. What I value about this program is that its design is aligned with classroom use, with resources and support dedicated to teacher-mediated activities. The *Story Jumper* website contains lessons plans that are linked to subject areas and events happening each month (e.g. Women's History Month in March). The story-making engine has a teacher management section, which allows teachers to view the books created by individual children in their class. The software was designed to support collaboration among children and it allows multiple people to edit the same book at the same time and video-chat with their co-authors.

https://www.storyjumper.com/

Storybird brands itself as a platform for writers, readers, and artists of all ages and is a fantastic resource for illustrated stories. The website curates illustrations and artwork that can be used in user-generated stories. *Storybird* can be used on any device, including touchscreens and desktop PCs. It has a dedicated section for educators and offers a classroom management option as well as tips aligned with the Core Curriculum. The illustrations can be used to inspire children's own picturebooks or even novels with older writers. The key premise of *Storybird* is that a story starts with pictures, which are used as prompts for children's own stories.

https://storybird.com/educators/

The *Times Educational Supplement* (TES) website offers a wealth of advice written by teachers for teachers. It contains detailed instructions for creating a digital book on *Storybird*.

https://www.tes.com/teaching-resource/easy-instructions-for-creating-a-free-ebook-on-storybird-11076810

Story Maker

This fantastic work by the British Council will be familiar to teachers across the world. *Story Maker*, available on the British Council's website, is a simple way of introducing children to story structures and story characters, with guided questions and prompts provided by *Story Maker*'s developers. Children can choose the type of story, props and characters' names and print the final story out. The focus is on children's learning of basic English vocabulary, so teachers interested in fostering agentic reciprocity will need to think creatively about the ways in which the tool can be embedded in their classrooms.

http://learnenglishkids.britishcouncil.org/en/games/story-maker

Little Bird Tales

Little Bird Tales is a subscription site with a choice of a school or home account. Paid membership includes the option for children to use their own photos, voiceovers, text and drawings to make their own digital stories.

https://www.littlebirdtales.com/info/premium/section/teacher/

My Story Book

My Story Book is suitable for the youngest age range: pre-schoolers and lower-primary-school children will enjoy it best. The user interface is very child-friendly, with large icons and pictorial navigation. Children can add 'items' and backgrounds to their own drawings and accompany these with their own texts or audio-recordings. Final stories can be printed out as a PDF (there is a nominal charge for each PDF) and stored in a library of stories. The software works for touchscreens and computers and requires log-in using an email address.

https://www.mystorybook.com/

The edition specifically created for schools is available for iPads and is called *My Story Book Creator School Edition*, available to download from here:

https://itunes.apple.com/gb/app/my-story-book-creator-school-edition/id449232368?mt=8

Scribjab

The program *Scribjab* is very popular in Canadian schools. It was created to support bilingual (English and French) story creation for both teacher and parent users. It runs as a website as well as iPad application, so it can be used on desktop PCs and iPads. Children can add their multilingual stories to the site, using their own drawings and texts. The user interface is less polished than those of the US sites, but the site has some very authentic stories created with the children's own drawings, which teachers and children may like to read. These stories are available from the 'read' section: http://scribjab.com/en/read/browse.html

I was drawn to this resource not so much by its technological affordances as by the philosophy behind its development. There is a direct synergy between the aims of the developers to support children's story-making and the aims pursued by Vivian Gussin Paley and our team in encouraging children's story authorship. If you read the approach followed by the Scribjab developers, you will notice the emphasis on open-ended story-making. For instance, they share our view 'that for children to feel that they OWN the books will be more important than strict grammatical accuracy or spelling'.

http://scribjab.com/en/about/tour.html

StoryKit

StoryKit is an iPhone app developed by the International Children's Digital Library (ICDL) Foundation. This app is for children beyond pre-school age who want to create their own e-books with photographs, text and some drawings.

https://itunes.apple.com/gb/app/storykit/id329374595?mt=8

There is currently no PC-based software dedicated to story-making for UK schools. (There used to be a fantastic program called *RealeWriter* but it has unfortunately been phased out.) For classrooms with iPads, the free application *Our Story* may be suitable.

Our Story

Our Story can be used for multimedia stories, since users can add their own pictures, texts and sounds. Finished stories can be sent to other users, played from the iPad or printed out as PDFs in three different formats. The app is free to use and its links to the App Stores are on the Open University website. I have been centrally involved in the app's development and conducted several studies with the app in its early stages. A summary of ideas for how to use the app can be found on the Open University website:

http://www.open.ac.uk/creet/main/projects/our-story

The apps and programs listed so far comply with the idea of open-ended story content and are aligned with the 5As philosophy. If you wish to support story-making with a more directive approach, then the following template-based story-making apps may be more suitable.

Toontastic

The *Toontastic* app is based on story templates and pre-designed props and advertised as a creative storytelling app. It allows children to create 3D cartoons using the app's set of characters, props and backgrounds. Children can add their drawings and narration to the stories and they can also animate them with 3D effects. The app is owned and administered by Google and available for free from a dedicated website: https://toontastic.withgoogle.com/

TikaTok

TikaTok is a tool for digital story-making developed by the international publishing house Pearson Ltd. *TikaTok* offers a range of templates in which children can insert their own texts and pictures. Children may like the ready-made frames and templates provided by the publisher. The website also offers resources for teachers: there are lesson plans developed in alignment with the US Common Core curriculum.

https://www.tikatok.com/learn/lessonPlan

Tuxpaint

If you wish to support children's story-making with drawings and arts, you may want to explore with them the digital drawing software *Tuxpaint*, which offers many templates and ready-made images for children's art-making. Children can access a variety of painting and drawing tools with a single tap. The free software supports the use of hundreds of photographic and cartoon images, including stamps, various types of paintbrushes etc., as well as 'magic' (special effects) tools. The magic tools produce aesthetic effects that couldn't be replicated on paper to the same effect, such as blurring parts of the image or making parts of an image look like a cartoon. The software is advertised as a computer literacy drawing activity for three- to twelve-year-olds and available for free from this website:

www.tuxpaint.org

Moving even further from the 5As of personalisation but recognising the multiple purposes we may have in supporting children's story-making, the next three resources are suited to specific school-related objectives.

Pobble

If a teacher wishes to correct children's grammar and assess their writing, then *Pobble* might be their choice (https://www.pobble.com/). *Pobble* is a very popular writing platform among UK teachers. It supports planning, sharing and assessing children's writing. Teachers can upload children's handwritten stories, and others can comment on them, as shown in this example:

https://www.pobble.com/works/d4dbb045

Comic Life

Comic Life can be used to create comic books using one's own photos. Children's comics can be enhanced with the *Comic Life* template that can add light effects or specific comic themes. There are individual frames where users can add their pictures and text. Finished stories can be printed out or saved in the digital library; the free version is only available for 30 days of use.

http://comiclife.com/

Wacky Web Tales

Wacky Web Tales are template- and text-based digital stories that users can customise with specific parts of speech, selected for each tale. The site is popular with teachers who wish to practise parts of speech with children and is curated by Houghton Mifflin's Education Place. Such template-supported story authoring is suitable for children who need some inspiration with their stories or simply want to have some fun. Teachers or children can choose a tale by selecting the story title and then add words as per the description of what the parts of speech might be. For example, in the story 'Pet Show', users are asked to insert pet name, body part, adjectives, plural noun, food, clothing, foreign-language singular noun and colours. The final story created through this process is then customised with the author's words.

http://www.eduplace.com/tales/

Apps for Good and App Inventor

I mentioned in Chapter 1 that the boundaries between digital books and apps are often blurred, especially when the digital books are full of interactive and multimedia features (and hence may be called 'story apps'). I conclude this chapter with two initiatives that position children as app-makers.

Apps for Good, according to their website, are currently in 400 schools, colleges and informal learning centres and they focus on 'creating mobile, social and web apps'. The initiative is aimed at slightly older children (beginning at ten) and is supported by volunteers who help teachers to support children in making their own apps. The community-oriented vision of the initiative resonates with the agency/reciprocity framework of personalisation.

https://www.appsforgood.org/public/get-involved

The App Inventor initiative at the Massachusetts Institute of Technology (MiT) is an example of how children can act as app evaluators as well as developers. The direct link to the pool of academics at MiT is an important quality assurance and sets an example of how universities can work with industry and public communities. The motto of the group – 'anyone can build apps that impact the world' – and the provision of app-development tools and guidance constitute exemplary practice in this area.

http://appinventor.mit.edu/explore/

Chapter summary

The concept of children as story authors is consistent with maker-centred learning pedagogy. The 5As of authorship, autonomy, authenticity, aesthetics and attachment encourage children's agency and position them as makers of their own contents. Adults can mediate children's creation of personal stories by listening actively and providing access to story-making programs that fit the story-making context and the children's needs. To support children's agency it is important that facilitation is guiding but not prescriptive. Adults need to reflect on the story prompts they use to encourage children's story-making as well as on the intended audience with whom the children's final stories will be shared. Several story-making apps are available for children's open-ended story-making. This chapter has listed a few that can be adopted for home, school and informal learning contexts.

Reflection point

> Nobody is a villain in their own story. We're all the heroes of our own stories. (George R. R. Martin)

I like this quote from the American novelist George R. R. Martin because it prompts me to think about the motivations behind the stories we create and propagate. I have seen many stories created by young children and can't remember a single one in which a child was presented as a bad character. Why is that so? If you were to produce a story as an adult, would you portray yourself as a villain? Reflect on these questions as you read the next two chapters dedicated to adults' story-making.

Further reading

'Digital' natives were first discussed in this widely cited – and contested – paper by Marc Prensky. You may find it interesting to read his argument and form your own view about it.

Prensky, M. (2001) 'Digital natives, digital immigrants part 1', *On the Horizon*, 9(5): 1–6.

Jerome Bruner's must-read book about the importance of stories in our lives:

Bruner, J. S. (2003) *Making Stories: Law, Literature, Life*. Cambridge, MA: Harvard University Press.

To find out more about the storytelling/story-acting approaches to the sharing of children's personal stories, I recommend exploring the MakeBelieve Arts Charity website:

http://www.makebelievearts.co.uk/helicopterstorieslettingimaginationfly/

These two seminal books discuss the storytelling/story-acting technique in more detail:

Lee, T. (2015) *Princesses, Dragons and Helicopter Stories: Storytelling and Story Acting in the Early Years*. London: Routledge.

Cremin, T., Flewitt, R., Mardell, B. & Swann, J. (eds) (2016) *Storytelling in Early Childhood: Enriching Language, Literacy and Classroom Culture*. London: Taylor & Francis.

If you are interested in reading more about the creativity angle on children's story-making with digital technologies, this book by Dr Sakr and early years educators might interest you:

Sakr, M., Federici, R., Hall, N., Trivedy, B. & O'Brien, L. (2018) *Creativity and Making in Early Childhood*. London: Bloomsbury.

If you are interested in maker-centred learning, you may find the following book useful. Be sure to check the accompanying website, which contains pedagogic tips and scenarios for teachers.

Clapp, E. P., Ross, J., Ryan, J. O. & Tishman, S. (2016) *Maker-Centered Learning: Empowering Young People to Shape Their Worlds*. London: John Wiley.

If the children you work with are skilled readers and writers and you are interested in supporting their blogging skills, you may find this short volume of interest:

Barrs, M. & Horrocks, S. (2014) *Educational Blogs and Their Effects on Pupils' Writing*. Reading: CfBT Education Trust.

7
Teachers as authors of children's digital books

In Chapter 6, I discussed the importance of supporting children's creation of their own stories and digital books. In this chapter I delegate the authorship to teachers. Having worked very closely with several teachers over the years, I am cautious about suggesting new activities and resources for their already very packed agenda and list of responsibilities. As it stands, the current UK curriculum does not place emphasis on media/digital/multimedia literacy and does not prepare teachers for teaching with and about new technologies. This textbook cannot plug the big hole. The focus on digital books is very specific. I hope, however, that my practical recommendations for using digital books will be a useful addition to advice on media literacy and technology use more broadly.

Cast your mind back to Chapter 5 and the multiple reasons for children to be story authors. There are many diverse reasons for teachers to be authors too. Teachers may wish to become authors of children's digital books because they want to position themselves as writers and makers in the classroom, because they want to make the books in their classrooms more meaningful and personalised for individual children, or perhaps because they want to convey a specific idea to children in a new medium.

I am particularly excited about the potential of digital books created by educational professionals to address the low quality of educational content available for children's digital reading and to become a means for teachers to share, innovate and contribute their own expertise and knowledge to children's reading on screen. There are many programs with which teachers can make their own digital books for, or with, children. Such self-created digital books offer flexible and low-cost options for publication and can contain a diverse range of authentic themes, plots and characters.

I begin this chapter with a theory- and literature-based rationale for why teachers' authorship of children's digital books matters. This is followed by some case study examples, recommendations of resources, and strategies to support teachers as authors and makers of children's digital books.

The importance of teachers' authorship of children's digital books

Teachers act as children's role models, agents of socialisation and brokers of knowledge. As such, teachers are uniquely positioned to author the books through which children assimilate knowledge and learn about human values. Teresa Cremin has written extensively about the ways in which teachers can position themselves as writers. Teachers who read and write and writers who read can model the practice of literacy, extend children's literacy life and encourage reading for pleasure (see e.g. Cremin et al. 2009). In this chapter, I extend the 'teachers as writers' proposition by suggesting that teachers can become the authors and multimedia makers of children's digital books. This means that teachers may not only provide the text for children's stories but also enrich them with images, audio-recordings and even interactivity. This may sound like an ambitious, perhaps daunting suggestion. But there is evidence that teachers are excellent multimedia story-makers and there are some easy-to-use software platforms facilitating teachers' creation of stories. Why should teachers engage in this practice?

Since the early 2010s, there has been a proliferation of new forms of children's stories (e.g. storybook apps, iBooks, enhanced e-books), available on a variety of reading platforms, including iPads, LeapReaders™ and Android tablets. However, despite greater availability of and access to digital stories, the quality and diversity of digital stories for young children are low. In Chapter 2, I outlined ways in which publishers and policy-makers could address this issue. In this chapter I propose that teachers can enrich children's digital books with educational content that directly connects to the lives of the children in their classroom. This can happen in partnerships with commercial producers and there are some companies and researchers that partner up with schools. Although not everyone is fortunate enough to be in a productive partnership, all teachers can choose to change the content of children's reading on screen. Any teacher can be a blogger and any teacher can be a digital story-maker. Teachers as authors can create digital books that extend specific topics or introduce new concepts. Such teacher-generated books can address a specific curriculum area and contain bespoke support for individual children. For example, in one UK classroom participating in my research, the teaching assistant created a digital book with words that contained consonant clusters to support children's early blending practice. The teaching assistant, while supporting a phonics lesson, noticed children's enthusiasm when using iPads but also that no suitable material was available for practising their phonics skills. She used the story-making app to make a simple story with each page dedicated to different consonant blends (e.g. 'glasses' and 'glue' on one page and 'dream' and 'dragon' on another page).

Teacher-created digital books may motivate children to take part in reading-related activities and also to find delight in stories.

Another key reason for teachers' involvement in story-making is the recurring evidence that children's literature (both digital and non-digital books) lacks socio-cultural, gender and ethnic diversity. In their choice of authors and their propagation of bestselling titles, many Anglo-American publishers reproduce dominant socio-cultural, ethnic and gender norms. The social media campaign #WeNeedDiverseBooks and the non-profit grassroots organisation We Need Diverse Books™ advocate 'essential changes in the publishing industry' (https://diversebooks.org/about-wndb/). Such changes are important but cannot happen overnight; teacher-led production of children's books could gradually contribute to shifting the mindset and enrich the canon of children's literature.

Stories made by teachers can build on the cultural background of the children in their classroom and the local context of the school. I have seen some lovely self-made books by teachers in a New Zealand classroom, which contained photos of the local park and words about plants and birds living there. Stories authored by teachers can also contain characters and plots that portray the readers in the classroom rather than being the idealised characters often propagated by commercial publishers. For instance, in one classroom in the English Midlands, the teacher decided to make children in her class the heroes of her fictional story, an idea that has motivated children to read the book over and over again.

Teachers can also create digital books that address a specific topic that they need to discuss with the children in their class, such as bullying or the importance of sharing. Presenting the topic in the form of a story will structure the topic in an accessible way and aid children's understanding and identification with the content.

Coming back to personalised learning, another important theme that can be conveyed to children through teacher-made digital books is the teacher's own life. Teachers can share with children some of their childhood memories, reading interests or hobbies and reconstruct the world of story as a space for conversation and mutual understanding of origins and shared presence. If we want to grow a generation of empathetic citizens, we need to introduce more opportunities for teachers to teach emotional skills; personal stories are an exemplary medium to do that. Why not create books for children which outline how their teacher grew up, how their teachers act in the local community, how they show acts of compassion? If children know their teachers as a person they will respect and appreciate them even more. In my UKLA minibook on personalisation (Kucirkova 2014b), I share an example of a teacher who created a digital book based on photographs depicting his typical weekend. The plot was fairly simple and the pictures were photographs of the teacher's garden and a few objects at home, but the children absolutely loved his story. The teachers in our project reported unexpected positive consequences from engaging in the process, including improved classroom dynamics.

Books that feature teachers as story heroes are definitely not common practice in mainstream schools, and the children read that book with great delight and interest. Providing such innovative content through the medium of a digital book may become an exciting way of refreshing children's reading lives and introducing more reciprocity into classrooms. Worth a try, perhaps?

Teachers and children creating digital books together

The continuum of agency and reciprocity reminds us that teachers' authorship of stories needs to be accompanied with an ongoing process of negotiating a shared perspective in the classroom. Reciprocity can take the form of direct collaboration and teachers' co-authorship of digital books with children. Through collaborative story-making, teachers and children can practise vital curriculum skills together and at the same time learn together about each other's stories. Whether the book is about the teacher, the child, or both, the process of creation can be an enjoyable back-and-forth negotiation of story events and characters. Digital books may be better suited to collaborative co-creation than print books, for three reasons.

Unlike print books, digital books remove established hierarchies between adult and child and open up several ways into a story. Digital books also offer flexibility of reproduction and content-sharing. Last but not least, the ease of including photographs and one's own drawings with a single tap is a significant advantage.

Teachers do not need to spend their free time making books for children; they can create digital books with the children in the classroom, as part of various lessons and methods of teaching set topics. In doing so, they can introduce children to the concepts of authorship, audience awareness and digital literacies, in *addition* to the specific topic they're teaching (e.g. studying the life of Henry VIII through collaborative multimedia story-making). A collaborative story-making process is likely to be followed by joint story-sharing, which can be a very rewarding and motivating experience for children-authors. Finished books can be shared on the interactive whiteboard and be part of a whole-class discussion. Alternatively, given that digital books can be easily reproduced electronically and customised for different children, teachers can produce individual digital books and either print them out or send them to children's individual accounts in the digital library.

In their personalisation theory developed in the context of adults' use of mobile phones, Oulasvirta and Blom (2008) argue that creating a shared object intensifies the experience of everyone involved. They argue that personalisation heightens the motivation of both the creator and the receiver. This reciprocal motivation is present in both personalising digital tools and personalised stories. The theory suggests that both teachers and children benefit from creating digital books together.

Strategies for creating digital books

To inspire your own approach to digital story-making for children, I outline three fictionalised case studies to illustrate how teachers and other educational professionals can enrich the curriculum with their own digital stories. The case studies are representative examples from several projects I have conducted with UK teachers in the past six years. The case studies did not happen exactly as I describe them and are not intended to be directly emulated; my intention is to ignite your own ideas regarding possible approaches.

Case study 1

Ben, a teacher in a Year 4 Key Stage 2 classroom (nine- to ten-year-olds), created a digital book to accompany his teaching of a history lesson. The lesson followed the National Curriculum's topic concerned with the lives of significant individuals who have contributed to national and international achievements. Ben decided to focus his book on Rosa Parks and

Emily Davison. He used the *Our Story* app to put together a set of pictures with text and sounds. He downloaded photographs, with appropriate attribution, from the Library of Congress, which has a comprehensive bank of resources on Rosa Parks:

https://www.loc.gov/rr/program/bib/rosaparks/rosaparks.html

He arranged the images in a chronological sequence of the key events in Parks's life and annotated them with short descriptive captions. For example, he used the Montgomery Sheriff's Department booking photo of Rosa Parks after she was arrested and annotated it with this caption: 'Rosa was arrested by the police and fined $14 for refusing to give up her bus seat for a white passenger.' He used the microphone feature to audio-record a longer version of the text and added the following voice-over to the picture:

> On the 1st of December 1955, Rosa Parks did something extraordinary and brave: she refused to disobey a bus driver's order to give up her seat to a white passenger. Rosa was seated in the coloured section of the bus and the white passenger was standing because the whites-only section was full. But Parks refused to give the white passenger her seat. It was not a simple act of disobedience but an act of resistance against bus segregation. There were some other American women who in the 1940s and 1950s refused to support bus segregation. Do you know who they were? Name one and add her picture and text to this story.

Ben uploaded the finished story to his Dropbox account and downloaded it on the individual iPads used by the children in his classroom. Now each child had a version of the book and could edit it in their own way. Children could choose whether to add Lillie Mae Bradford or Irene Morgan (or others) to complete the story their teacher had started.

Ben also inserted some personalisation features into the digital story: he left some blank pages for children to complete. In the middle of the digital book, he inserted a profile picture of Rosa Parks and the following text: 'Imagine you are Rosa Parks. Make an audio-recording about what happened on the 1st of December. You can add your own photo to the page. Use the iPad camera to take your picture.'

He inserted an image of a golden photoframe into three pages/slides of the story and encouraged children to add photos or names of their classmates. These pages were preceded with the following voiceover: 'Rose Parks is a heroine who is remembered for how she showed courage, forgiveness and hope. Who in our class is an example of courage?'

The next photo frame had the title 'Hope' and this audio-recorded instruction by the teacher: 'Who is our classroom hero of Hope?' On the next page: 'Who is our example of Forgiveness? Take a nice photo of your heroes and heroines and add them to the three photo frames.'

Children completed their digital stories with great enthusiasm, working either individually or in pairs. At the end of the activity, they shared the finished stories with each other. Ben also selected some examples to display on the interactive whiteboard. He was interested in seeing how children responded to the story of Rosa Parks but also in how they related her life to their own. He praised children's efforts to recognise valuable characteristics in their classmates and suggested they make a display based on a 'Hall of Fame' with pictures of children displaying the three virtues of hope, courage and forgiveness. The activity was a well-accomplished amalgam of personal/social and past/present connections to stories.

Case study 2

Gabbie, an early years practitioner in a Steiner kindergarten, created a series of digital picture-based dictionaries and personal stories using *Our Story*. The digital dictionaries were photographs of objects in the school, such as a fork next to a plate or a washbasin in the bathroom. Each photo was accompanied with the word in capitals – e.g. 'SPOON' – and Gabbie's audio-recorded pronunciation of the word. She used the digital dictionary with children whose first language was not English or who had weaker language skills when they started attending the pre-school.

The personal stories she created were about individual children in the class. The stories were all titled '[first name of the child]'s Day' and followed the child's day in the kindergarten. The pictures were photos of the individual children and the text was written by the teacher (there was no audio-recording in these digital stories). For example, Matthew's story had eight pages, whose text I reproduce with permission and fictionalised children's names:

- Page 1 started with a photo of Matthew waving goodbye to his grandma in the morning. The text read, 'Bye-bye granny, have a lovely day!'
- Page 2 featured a photo of Matthew playing with wooden blocks with another boy in a corner of the classroom. The caption was, 'Matthew is playing with his friend Frank. Sharing toys is good.'
- Page 3 was a photo of Matthew eating grapes from a colourful plastic bowl: 'Matthew is enjoying his morning snack. Yummy!'

HOW AND WHY TO READ AND CREATE CHILDREN'S DIGITAL BOOKS

- Page 4 was a photo of Matthew playing outside with a giant party bubble: 'Matthew loves bubbles more than anything in the world!'
- Page 5 showed Matthew eating peas with a girl sitting next to him: 'Matthew likes eating vegetables. Vegetables are good for our bodies!'
- Page 6 featured Matthew reading a book: 'Psst, it's reading time! Matthew is reading Rabbit & Bear!'
- Page 7 was a selfie of Gabbie with Matthew, both looking into the camera with a broad smile: 'Gabbie and Matthew always have a lot of fun together!'
- Page 8 was a quick shot of Matthew putting on a coat in the class-room corridor: 'It's time to go home. See you tomorrow Matthew!'

Gabbie printed the children's stories on coloured paper and folded and stapled them into A6 format. The children were encouraged to take their printed copies home and share them with their parents. Some families requested a digital copy and so Gabbie sent an electronic copy of the digital book to the parents' email address. There was not a single child in the class who didn't love their personalised book. Gabbie's books became a tradition in the kindergarten, each cohort of new children receiving their own personalised books created by the teachers.

Case study 3

Key stage 2 teacher Rebecca created a digital story to bring closer to students one of the statutory requirements in the Year 3 science curriculum: the life cycle of plants. The UK curriculum demands that pupils be able to 'iden-tify and describe the functions of different parts of flowering plants: roots, stem/trunk, leaves and flowers, as well as understanding the requirements of plants for life and growth': https://www.gov.uk/government/publica-tions/national-curriculum-in-england-science-programmes-of-study

Rebecca decided to create a fictional multimedia story about an imag-inary girl called Rebecca, who follows the life path of a plant in her own garden. She purposefully made the character a younger version of herself because she could easily take pictures of herself in the garden and because it would help the children to take the role of storyteller. Instead of giving chil-dren a ready-made book, she made it into a 'living book' that the children could add to and complete during the classroom activity of story-making/story-sharing. To create the book, the teacher used her classroom laptop and PowerPoint slides and the free art-making software *Tuxpaint*.

To begin her digital story, Rebecca took a selfie standing in an allotment with bare soil. There were several tools lying around on the ground but no sign of flowers or other plants. She added the following text: 'Rebecca wonders how to make her garden bloom. Can you help her?'

The teacher showed children this digital page (slide) on the interactive whiteboard and asked the children, 'Can you help Rebecca with her garden?'

They enthusiastically answered with a loud 'Yes!!'

'What does Rebecca need to do to make her plants grow?' the teacher asked.

Various answers came up. Rebecca repeated the most relevant ones: 'Good answer, some sunshine. Get some tools. Very good. So which tools will Rebecca need to start the work?'

Instead of the children verbally describing the tools, Rebecca asked them to draw them on the interactive whiteboard. She clicked on *Tuxpaint* (the software was installed on her laptop connected to the whiteboard) and opened a blank canvas with a set of paintbrushes. She called individual children to come forward and draw the tools they thought she would need to plant the garden seeds. A boy drew a shovel, a girl used a digital stamp (or sticker) of a sun (available from the drawing software tool) and another girl drew a watering can and soil.

The teacher thanked the children and saved their pictures as three JPG images on her laptop and inserted them into the photo gallery connected to the *Our Story* app. She then asked a different group of children to come forward to the board and continue the digital story with the depicted tools. She instructed them to write in the 'correct tense' and type up their short sentences next to the individual tools. The final pages for the classroom story were:

- Page 2: 'The sun was shining.'
- Page 3: 'Rebecca used a shovel to dig a hole.'
- Page 4: 'She watered the soil with a watering can.'
- Page 5: 'She planted a seed in the soil.'

The lesson ended but Rebecca continued work with the 'living book' the next day. The lesson began with her displaying the incomplete digital story on the interactive whiteboard. She swiped through the first five pages and asked the class, 'And what happens next? Rebecca planted a seed in the soil. What will happen to the seed in the soil?' She waited for children's answers and then suggested they act out the 'life cycle of the seed' with their own bodies. The teacher orchestrated the story dramatisation as a whole-class activity. Children gathered on the carpet in the centre of the classroom and acted out how the seed would grow, following Rebecca's instructions. She encouraged them by asking, 'Can you show me what a seed looks like?' The children crouched and lay on the floor, pretending to look very small. She then asked them to pretend to be a seed that was receiving a lot of rain and sunshine. 'Now can you show me what a shoot looks like?' The children jumped up and raised their arms up in the air. 'And if I give you more water how will you grow?'

Rebecca took pictures of children acting out the story and occasionally had to shush them because they were getting very excited. 'Excellent, now can you show me what grown-up plants look like? And when it's time to blossom can you all turn into flowers? Nice smiling flowers!' The children were beaming with joy. 'Wonderful, well done! What about your roots? And your leaves?' The children used their hands to indicate wiggling leaves and their feet to represent the firm roots of the plant. Rebecca took pictures of children pretending to be the individual plant parts, selecting either a wide shot featuring several children or an individual child who was acting particularly persuasively. She used the iPad camera to take the pictures, so the pictures were part of the photo gallery, ready to be used to continue the story. When the acting part was finished, Rebecca connected her iPad to the whiteboard and opened the *Our Story* app to display the photo gallery together with the storyboard. (Please make sure that when taking photographs of children you have their parents' explicit permission and the children's verbal consent to do so.)

Rebecca then said to the class, 'My story doesn't seem to be in the right order. Can you order the images in the right sequence?' She called individual children forward to select pictures and drag them into suitable positions on the storyboard to create a sequence. The activity continued with annotations of the individual pictures in the digital story as well as with pens and pencils in children's workbooks. In sum, the use of the app in this activity facilitated children's active involvement in producing the pictures and text for the story and thereby connected their own bodies to the plant life cycle.

Apps and programs for creating digital stories

Teachers' choice of story-making apps/programs will be dictated by their familiarity with a particular technology and its availability in their classroom. The following list provides some examples of programs teachers may find useful. In comparison with the programs outlined in Chapter 6, the user interface of these story-making programs is more oriented towards adults, with text-based navigation, possibilities to enlarge the text for display on the interactive whiteboard, and adult settings that require email and/or credit card registration. The programs give expression to text rather than images or videos and can be used by adults together with children or by adults or older children independently.

Story-making on laptops and desktop PCs run by Microsoft

Teachers are very likely to be familiar with Microsoft Power Point but they may not be familiar with its use for story-making. PowerPoint functionality is available with any Microsoft package installed on a laptop or desktop PC. When creating a presentation, you can think of it as creating a book, the individual slides corresponding to book pages.

To make a story, arrange the slides in a chronological order and combine pictures with text. You can easily insert images stored on your computer and also add sounds and video files. Video and audio files can be added using the 'insert' option on each individual slide. If the slides represent book pages, it is important to allow enough space between the text and the pictures. When I create a digital book in PowerPoint, my pages typically look like the example in Figure 7.1.

The finished book can be exported as a PDF, which can be printed in various sizes or as booklets, depending on your printer. It can also

'Do you think there is an animal missing in this picture? Why?'

Figure 7.1 An example of a PowerPoint story page.
Source: Author

be saved and shared as a multimedia story with sounds and video. If you want a final digital story with multimedia, you will need to save it as a MPEG or Windows Media Video (.wmv) file. The story will then play in one loop and you can adjust the display timings of individual slides with the 'animations' options.

If you want to print the story out, you need to save it as a PDF and print the pages, which will then need folding and stapling. You can also format it as a booklet during the book creation process. A step-by-step guide to how to create a booklet and print it out may be found here:

http://www.thewindowsclub.com/create-booklet-book-microsoft-word

I have described here the simplest way of using PowerPoint for a digital or printed story but Microsoft offers several more sophisticated options. If you are interested in exploring them further, I suggest you conduct an online search using keywords relating to the specific format you are after (e.g. 'Microsoft booklet A3'). Given that Microsoft Office has a large user base, there are many free guides and even video tutorials on YouTube which may guide you in what you want to do.

As well as with programs for computers, you can create a digital book with tablet applications. These apps are predominantly for picture-driven stories; I described the most popular ones in the last chapter. For adults and older children's story-making *Book Creator* may be suitable.

Story-making on tablets and iPads

Book Creator One 4+ and *Book Creator for iPad* by Red Jumper Ltd are the most popular apps for creating multimedia books on iPads. Users can add music, narration, video, text and pictures and save finished stories in a digital library. The app can be purchased through Apple's Volume Purchase Programme with a discount.

https://itunes.apple.com/app/id661166101?mt=8&&referrer=click%3D405de7be-0b94-4cce-816e-c57a818badde

Publishing professionally designed books

For teacher-authors who wish to take their books into the international marketplace and earn royalties from book sales, it may be worth researching the options available to independent authors. A popular platform is BookRix. BookRix is a free self-publishing platform that offers e-book distribution services to independent writers: https://www.bookrix.com/

Another commercial site is Amazon's Self-Publishing on Demand service. Amazon is behind the reader device Kindle, so its self-publishing services focus on books that can be read on Kindle. However, it also offers the opportunity to sell printed copies (on demand) with the CreateSpace facility (which at the time of writing was merging with Kindle Direct Publishing to form one service: https://kdp.amazon.com/en_UK/). A guide video and details are available here:

https://www.amazon.co.uk/p/feature/78e7r2e8ccbv3sp

Young Storyteller

I have mentioned the option of digital books that are co-created by or made independently by older children. Children's own creation is largely facilitated by the Amazon's Young Storyteller programme. In the UK, Amazon collaborates with the National Literacy Trust, which allows teachers to sign up and access resources to support story-making. Adults or children can write stories to make a book and then have the book published as a paperback or e-book and sell it on the Amazon website. The school then receives the royalties from book sales. More about this programme is available from:

www.amazon.co.uk/youngstoryteller

Photo books

For teachers who feel especially creative and wish to create professional-looking books that can be sold online, there are some professional book-making tools that can be used to create printed photo books, picturebooks and even novels and magazines. All of these services carry a fee and are not particularly designed for use in schools but could be adapted. Examples include:

Blurb
http://www.blurb.co.uk/bookmaking-tools

Shutterfly
https://www.shutterfly.com/

Solentro
For UK customers the shipping costs are lower for photo books made by Solentro, since it is a UK-based provider.

https://www.solentro.co.uk/

This site provides specific offers for educators, though it is currently only available for US teachers.

https://www.bookemon.com/

Create My Books

This site has multiple book-building functions and is suitable for books that are more text than photo driven.

https://www.createmybooks.com/BE/en/

Bear in mind that the key market of these companies comprises users interested in creating photo books, so they are well suited for teachers who wish to create polished picturebooks and have access to their own (high-quality) photographs. Some sites offer discounts for educators (and Bookemon allows you to order books using official purchase orders) and some offer discounts for bulk orders. The story-making process happens in the 'create mode', where users can upload existing book pages or start creating them from scratch using the provider's templates. Most sites allow one to upload Word, PDF and PowerPoint files, so you can prepare the story using the tools you are familiar with. You can also choose a pre-designed template and insert your story into colourful photo frames with seasonal or occasion-relevant themes (e.g. autumn leaves or celebration confetti). To print the book, you need to choose the format, cover and binding. Some providers offer the option of e-books in addition to print books and some will also help with ISBN registration if you want to obtain one for your book. The price per copy depends on the number of copies and delivery charges.

Chapter summary

This chapter has outlined rationales, strategies and resources for teachers interested in authoring digital stories for children in their classes. Digital books made by teachers can be treasure troves of useful information, local knowledge and authentic stories. The key reasons for teachers to create or co-create digital books for and with the children are: to contribute to making better-quality educational content available for children's on-screen reading; to enrich story diversity, including cultural and local knowledge; to provide bespoke support for individual children via stories; and to connect to the children in their classrooms by positioning themselves as writers, makers and three-dimensional human beings. The case studies outlined in this chapter illustrate the creative ways in which teachers can leverage the potential of digital books to motivate children to read and to connect their multimedia materials with the worlds of stories.

Reflection point

> I think of children's books as not so much for children, but as the filling that goes between the child and the adult world. One way or another, all children's books have to negotiate that space. (Michael Rosen)

This quote from the popular British children's writer Michael Rosen always makes me imagine a bridge built by books between adults and children. When writing for children, adults need to bridge between young readers' understanding and one's own conceptualisation of the world. At the same time, they need to strive for originality and to impart educational and moral guidance. This is not an easy task. When I was trying to write a children's book, I did not go down the typical route of reading many published children's books. Instead I spent countless hours talking to children about their own stories. I also found children's reviews of books a great source of inspiration.

Bestselling children's authors have attractive websites which are a great place to learn about children's perspectives on specific titles. For example, the official site for the Harry Potter series (Pottermore) hosts a book club for Harry Potter fans. When logged in as a user, you can contribute your views and read other readers' views on the characters and plot twists. This can be a source of inspiration for your own writing, but also a way of getting to know the 'filling' between adults and children's story worlds.

Further reading

McCannon, D., Thornton, S. & Williams, Y. (2008) *The Encyclopedia of Writing and Illustrating Children's Books: From Creating Characters to Developing Stories, a Step-by-Step Guide to Making Magical Picture Books*. Philadelphia: Allen & Unwin. This encyclopaedia is a comprehensive guide to all the steps involved in developing, illustrating, writing, crafting and selling children's books. It will be of particular interest to teachers who decide to take the authorship of children's books to the next level and attempt large-scale distribution. The tips on how to adjust the content to different age groups and different book genres (comics, fantasy, fairy tales) may be particularly helpful for teachers-authors.

https://www.allenandunwin.com/browse/books/general-books/writing-language/The-Encyclopedia-of-Writing-and-Illustrating-Childrens-Books-Desdemona-McCannon-Sue-Thornton-Yadzia-Williams-9781741755152

Kucirkova, N. (2014) *iPads and Tablets in the Classroom: Personalising Children's Stories*. Leicester: UKLA. This resource offers practical examples of incorporating digital books created with *Our Story* into classrooms across year groups and subject areas.
http://www.ukla.org/publications/view/ipads_and_tablets_in_the_classroom_personalising_childrens_stories/

For teachers interested in building or strengthening their identity as a writer, the Teachers as Writers project run by the Arvon Foundation, the Open University and Exeter University may provide inspiration, particularly the engaging blogs written by participating teachers and researchers.
http://www.teachersaswriters.org/

Teachers who are story authors are creative and curious and may therefore find the *National Geographic* website inspiring. There is a section dedicated to teaching resources which has a wealth of story ideas and story sparks.
https://www.nationalgeographic.org/education/teaching-resources/

8

Parents as authors of children's digital books

The most natural, and historically oldest, form of children receiving stories from family members is oral storytelling, the stories being shared by older relatives with the younger generation. Today's families do not routinely share stories around a fire, but many have developed their own story-sharing routines. I remember my aunt telling my cousins a story every night before they went to bed. She invented the fictional character Eric, who had all the attributes of well-behaving boys. Eric would help with household chores and go to bed early. His good behaviour was rewarded with magical things that happened to him in my auntie's stories. If you are a parent you may share stories with your children, or you may remember the stories your parents and grandparents shared with you. In this chapter I want to build on this experience and extend the storytelling practice to story-making with digital technologies. I will try to convince you that stories that are written and/or illustrated and then captured in audio-recordings not only capture memories and experiences but can also extend them as a multimedia artefact that can be shared and archived for posterity.

The suggestion that parents be book authors is intended to enrich, not replace, parents' role as readers and co-readers of existing books and brokers of literature to their children. Equally, my emphasis on parents' story-*making* should not be taken to mean that this activity should substitute oral storytelling. Both story-reading and storytelling are unique activities in their own right; story-making with digital tools can unfold additional aspects of families' existing story-sharing routines. The rationale for involving parents in creating digital books for their child can be substantiated in various ways; let me mention two key benefits that I have observed in my work: those of preserving and celebrating dual-language proficiency and of facilitating positive shared use of digital technologies at home. I focus on digital books that can be created by parents for their children or together with the children.

Parents know their children's likes, needs and desires; they are the children's first and foremost role models, educators, caregivers and mentors. These multiple roles and this intimate knowledge of their children's lives make parents ideal candidates for crafting the content of books their children read. I use the generic word 'parents' throughout this chapter, but you may substitute it with any family members who are close to the child, including uncles, aunts, cousins or grandparents, as well as primary caregivers who may not be the child's biological parents but act as their guardians.

Similarly to the previous chapters, I begin with some broader guidance on how story-making can be supported, focusing on the method of story-prompting. This is followed by examples and useful resources. Given the focus on parents, I do not follow a specific pedagogy, but I emphasise the agency–reciprocity continuum that is common to all story-making.

Story-making in families: the whys and hows

How, where and why parents share stories with their children are as varied as the stories they tell each other. The stories can be autobiographical or fictional or a combination of the two. They can be a rare experience or a regular morning routine. For adults who are unfamiliar with story-sharing with children or would like more guidance on how to get started, I would recommend this freely available comprehensive guide written by the storytelling expert Steve Killick and Maria Boffey. The guide was written specifically for foster parents but it can be used by all parents.

https://www.thefosteringnetwork.org.uk/sites/www.fostering. net/files/content/building-relationships-through-storytelling-31-10-12. pdf

As explained in the guide, the key reason for storytelling in families is to build strong bonds and attachment between adults and children. Sensitive storytelling can also be part of emotional healing, particularly if there is a trusting relationship between the parent and child and they can use the story as a way of imagining alternative endings to a difficult experience. It can also be part of building a repertoire of shared stories and reference points (as with my aunt's Eric stories). Not all parents are natural-born storytellers, but the more parents share stories with their children, the more they discover that thousands of fantasy creatures and storylines lie dormant within both themselves and their children. Everyday occurrences can often awaken the stories within us and I would therefore be cautious about suggesting a specific model for story-sharing for all families. In a globalised world, we often underestimate the distinct socio-cultural practices in different families, which are often reflected in their stories. What educators, community workers and librarians can do is encourage story-making as one way of connecting children and parents around a shared artefact (a digital book). They can draw on some examples of digital books to demonstrate the benefits of this practice.

I often begin my conversations about this with parents by pointing out that many successful children's authors began their writing careers by writing a book for their own children first. One never knows who the next Julia Donaldson will be. In Kucirkova (2014a), I describe the experiences of two mums who became successful published authors by first writing a book for their own child:

https://theconversation.com/how-to-be-a-publishing-parent-and-help-diversify-childrens-literature-28744

After discussing some examples, I then tell parents about the research that shows that parents who create or co-create books in their own language feel more empowered to contribute to their children's education and report greater interest in sharing books with them at home (Janes & Kermani 2001). This research builds on the rich empirical work nested within the notion of 'funds of knowledge'.

Funds of knowledge in families

An approach that valorises and validates children's cultural heritage in a wider sense, beyond the linguistic focus, is known as 'funds of knowledge'. Funds of knowledge are 'the essential cultural practices and bodies of knowledge and information that households use to survive, to get ahead, or to thrive' (Moll 1992, p. 21). Moll, Amanti, Neff and Gonzalez (1992) studied in detail how children's funds of knowledge bridge homes and schools in diverse communities; their work brought to life a mosaic of family practices and linguistic, social and physical artefacts. Self-made books, photos and written stories are very much part of these multicultural, multilingual rivers of knowledge about self and others. Parents who wish to create digital books to promote their children's use of their native language, or to foster dual or bilingual communication, can usefully draw on the principles of funds of knowledge. I encourage you to think about the following examples in light of this philosophy.

The importance of parents as story-makers

Parents as language brokers

One key reason for encouraging parents to create digital books is to address the limited story content in local/minority languages and to increase children's access to content that is meaningful to them and celebrates their heritage. This suggestion is closely related to the issue of multilingualism and native languages and recognises parents' unique position as mediators of language and culture to their children.

From an educator's perspective, the increased migration and transnational movements in the twenty-first century have presented a complex array of issues for schools and local communities. The concentration of diverse languages in small geographical locations is one of them. Multicultural and multi-ethnic classrooms have become the norm rather than the special case of urban schools. State school curricula are only slowly adapting to the linguistic diversity available within the bilingual, immigrant, refugee and indigenous-minority communities they serve. The first language of children from these communities is rarely the language spoken by the majority. These children's native language is therefore often described as a 'minority language' or 'second language', or in the case of indigenous children 'heritage language'. There are rarely appropriate linguistic and socio-cultural resources for all children in diverse classrooms, and very few in the form of digital books, as documented by Sari, Takacs and Bus (2017). One way of addressing this problem is to encourage parents to create books for their children, in their own native language, and to share them with the school and wider communities.

You may ask why it is important to have digital books available in minority languages and what is wrong with books being available only in the majority language. Whereas the production costs of digital books, such as those created with the free *Our Story* app, are minimal, there are costs involved in translation and in producing printed versions of children's books. Digital books made by parents for their children can help to preserve the minority language in both written and spoken form. Moreover, if they narrate stories of local communities, they preserve and propagate local cultural heritage. The digital format can easily accommodate bilingual and multilingual versions, with flexible combinations of text and audio-narration in one or other language. Multilingualism celebrated through literary materials is an important means of fostering children's awareness of pluralism and multiculturalism. Therefore, a broader answer to the 'why?' question would be that it is essential for children's cultural understanding and intellectual learning to support bilingualism and multilingualism. The globalised world and the need for cross-cultural dialogue to maintain peace make that aim self-evident.

Jim Cummins from University of Toronto wrote an influential essay (2005) on 'strategies for recognizing heritage language competence as a learning resource within the mainstream classroom', in which he outlines how the educational field has advanced in relation to understanding and communicating the value of children's heritage language. Now that many scholars are challenging monolingual instructional approaches, heritage-language education is an established research field (see Brinton et al. 2017).

As for the cognitive advantage of multilingualism, research shows that children who are multilingual have several cognitive advantages over their monolingual peers, notably in terms of working memory and executive control (see Poarch & van Hell 2012; Engel de Abreu et al. 2012). Moreover, research shows that children interact differently when using digital books that are in English and ones in their native language. Christ, Wang and Erdemir (2018) investigated this issue in two classrooms that used iPads for a 'buddy reading' initiative. In the study, children read one book together in pairs. The study was conducted in parallel in the US and Turkey, with 27 US five- to six-year-olds and 28 Turkish four- to five-year-olds. The digital books used by the researchers were selected on the basis of their suitability for supporting children's language development; they highlighted text when read out or offered an alternative explanation of its meaning. In total, 12 digital books were read (each was read twice) across the school year. The importance of children accessing content in their native language became apparent when the Turkish children used their digital books in paired reading: the children collaborated and discussed the content only with the digital books written in Turkish. With the English-language digital books, the Turkish children engaged in what the researchers described as hotspot-centric behaviour, that is, the children merely tapped on the areas of the screen that were automatically highlighted for them. Unlike in previous research by the same team which documented buddy reading of print texts, when the children read the digital books in their native language they did not interact in a tutor–tutee style. Their engagement was collaborative and less hierarchical – a pattern we observed also in the context between a parent and a child reading a digital book together at home (Kucirkova, Sheehy & Messer, 2015).

To reiterate perhaps an obvious point, bilingualism, multilingualism, second-language acquisition and heritage education are complex research fields and the educational, linguistic and cultural situation of children cannot be remediated with a single solution such as parents creating their own digital books. Culture, income and language combine in complex ways in parents' approaches to education. Small interventions, such as creating digital books, need to take account of this. The positive experience of presenting a story in one's native language is not confined to bilingual or multilingual children, of course. Books made by parents for their children can be enjoyed by all families.

Parents as literacy brokers

Some successful research-based projects demonstrate the importance of parents' involvement in their children's literacy. The Parents as Literacy Supporters (PALS) family literacy programme is an inspiring example informed by rich research and is successfully used in several schools in British Columbia, Canada. PALS is aimed at parents and children aged between four and five years. The programme was developed by Jim Anderson and his colleagues at the University of British Columbia and is being implemented in several Canadian school districts. The approach involves two-hour sessions led by two facilitators, focusing on various literacy themes. All sessions begin with a shared meal, which is followed by an explanation of the literacy topic by the facilitator, discussion, hands-on activities with the children, debriefing and sharing resources. Emphasis is placed on learning through play and a sensitive approach to the unique cultural and linguistic background of the participants. One of the PALS sessions focuses on participants making their own books in their own languages. These are not digital books but paper-based books, using cuttings from newspapers and magazines or participants' own photos for illustrations. Books collaboratively produced by parents and children play a core role in programmes such as PALS to broker home–school relationships.

Another research-led project that originated in Canada and has been successfully implemented in Canadian provinces is the 'identity texts' story-making project. With its bilingual communities such as Quebec, Canada has a rich tradition of self-made bilingual resources. Professor Cummins and his colleague Judith Bernhard refer to self-made books as 'identity texts' and highlight that dual-language books represent not only an important literacy resource but also an identity-related object. Identity texts are often co-created by parents and children and are a beautiful example of how several literacies (written, visual, cultural, social and personal) can come together in a story.

Parents as technology brokers

My focus on digital stories positions parents not only as storytellers and story authors but also as story designers and technology mediators and coaches. The latter role is often discussed in relation to teachers and their technology skills, but parents play, especially in the case of young children, a dominant role, through both passive modelling of technology habits and active encouragement. Parents who use story-making apps to make stories for their children model for them that apps can be used to generate content and that this content can be personalised and culturally responsive. Digital books could be perceived as superior to print books in their *potential* to carry multiple languages and multiple means of story representation.

However, not all parents will want to create books in the digital medium; indeed, there is a known resistance among parents towards reading and using digital books with their children. A national survey in the UK found that most parents prefer to read print books to their children, especially in bedtime reading (Kucirkova & Littleton 2016). The reasons are multiple but a major force in play is parents' attitudes towards technology and young children. Many parents perceive digital books as part of children's screen time, which they want to minimise rather than increase. As I explained in Chapter 3, one of the most effective strategies to overcome such screen time concerns is to focus on active co-use of technology by parents and children. I described the reciprocity necessary for rich co-authorship of stories by adults and children in Chapter 7 in relation to teachers, and this applies equally to parents. When parents and children co-create digital books together, they learn about each other's technology skills: they can discuss the story plot, take pictures of their surroundings, audio-record voiceovers and involve as many senses and movements as possible in the activity. When parents make their own digital books for children, they do not need to add interactive or multimedia features; it is the combination of their personal experience and language (expressed in any mode) that will engage their children.

Some research studies show that encouraging parents and children to make digital books together supports positive parent–child joint use of technologies. For example, Sung and Siraj-Blatchford (2014) introduced the *Our Story* app to parents attending public libraries in Taiwan. The researchers used the app in three libraries and five workshops with parents over five months in 2013. They encouraged parents to co-create digital books with their children and documented several benefits for the child (e.g. children's increased confidence as a result of recording their own story), as well as joint parent–child benefits, such as increased dialogue and mutual enjoyment of using technologies together.

Parents as story editors

Thus far, I've described parents' story authorship in relation to open-ended stories, that is, stories whose content is decided entirely by the parent. It could be, however, that a parent decides to edit and customise an existing digital story rather than create their own from scratch. This practice can have similar benefits to those mentioned so far. For example, parents can translate existing digital stories into their native language using the Storyweaver platform (https://storyweaver.org.in/). Similarly, they can show children how to add their own illustrations to existing audio-books, thereby practising digital and media literacies with their children. What's more, digital books customised by parents for their children can be used as a fresh ingredient in families' existing reading routine. Sharing books in families using a one-to-one parent–child model has been heralded as exemplary practice to inculcate literacy in children and foster parent–child bonding. Millions of parents have read to their children from a young age, especially at bedtime. It should not be assumed, however, that shared reading is routine in all families or that all parents and children enjoy reading books together. Elaine Reese (2012) rightly points out that the idyllic experience of book reading portrayed in the media and some research studies is not the reality of all families. For some families shared reading can be quite a trial. In contrast, parent–child reading of self-made stories, or stories personalised for individual children, on an iPad could be perceived in a different light because of the coexistence of three factors: the motivational aspect of personalisation (i.e. stories that resonate with the readers); shared use of a device known to interest children; and parents' involvement in the production of the stories. Moreover, digital stories edited by parents for their children could supplement traditional book-reading routines that it may not be possible to keep. For example, some parents may be absent from shared reading sessions but they could prepare a digital book for their children which contains their voice. With apps such as *Me Books* (http://madeinme.com/me-books/), parents can add their own audio-recording to existing stories; with digital books such as *Mr Glue Stories* (http://mrgluestories.com/), children can add their own drawings and parents their own texts to existing stories. The playful and potentially boundary-free mix and match of digital stories is an unprecedented opportunity to foster reading for pleasure in families.

Strategies and examples to encourage parents' digital story-making

Although many parents will want to share and celebrate their socio-cultural heritage or promote dual-language use or positive parent–child interactions with technology, not all parents will be motivated to seek these benefits using digital books. This is where the mediating and mentoring role of educators comes in. In my and my colleagues' research, the encouragement of parents has come most often from teachers but also from local librarians, community workers and researchers.

Teachers may encourage parents to get involved in producing books for their children by presenting them with the reasons and ideas in this chapter. Alternatively, teachers may inspire parents to get involved in the teachers' own book production, as described in Chapter 7. Teachers can also suggest that parents and children co-create digital books at home for the children to share at school. Initiatives such as Parents As Literacy Supporters show that parent-oriented workshops run at schools are an effective way of involving parents in their children's literacy. Schools can partner up with local libraries and use the library premises to run sessions with parents. The teacher's supporting and facilitating role is particularly salient for families who may not have a tradition of shared reading or the use of technologies at home, or for families who are unfamiliar with the dominant culture of instruction in a new country and need encouragement and valorisation of their knowledge and socio-cultural heritage.

There are several ways in which teachers and educational professionals can contextualise the idea of parents' digital story-making. To indicate the possibilities, I present one illustrative example, the Brilliant Stories project, which has successfully engaged parents in creating digital multimedia books in a culturally diverse community in London.

Brilliant Stories

The Brilliant Stories project has produced a treasure trove of resources that are freely available from the project website and may be helpful to teachers or community leaders in engaging parents as authors of children's digital books. You can access the Brilliant Stories Community Educator Resource Pack for the Parent/Carer Learning Champions' Programme from:

https://somebrilliantstories.wordpress.com/

The initiative took place in the London Borough Haringey in 2013 and was funded through a grant from the Skills Funding Agency (UK government agency that funds further education and skills projects), supported by a group of experts in storytelling called Raising Voices. The project's overall objectives were:

1. To engage disadvantaged parents and carers in family learning through the use of digital technology and supported learning activities.
2. To improve the skills and literacy in digital technology of local adult learning tutors and community educators.
3. To increase access to further learning and development opportunities for parents and carers.
4. To create a pool of Parent/Carer Learning Champions committed to promoting inter-generational learning to other parents, carers and children.

The project is directly relevant to the content of this chapter in its objective to support family learning with digital technologies, encouraging parents to act as language and culture brokers and make their own digital stories. The Brilliant Stories team describes the creation of digital books in terms of 'multimedia learning journeys'; these were digital books created with *Our Story,* using the text, pictures and voiceovers of the participating parents. The project had a structure of 10 sessions, with pre-designed activities for the adult coordinators and trainers. The actual creation of the stories with the app didn't occur until Session 4 and was preceded by sessions in which the participants learnt how to operate tablets and cameras and brainstormed ideas about what makes a good story. These are important topics to cover with parents before story-making and are worth consideration by teachers/librarians who wish to facilitate parents' involvement in digital book production and children's use of technology more broadly. The parents participating in Brilliant Stories were also trained in how to take pictures with the tablet and how to story-board their ideas before creating the digital story. The story creation then involved the following steps:

- develop a story concept;
- prepare a storyboard using a paper-based template;
- take photos of objects that you would like to feature in the story;
- add text and voiceovers to accompany each picture;
- sequence individual pages and save the story.

It is worth pointing out that the focus in Brilliant Stories instructions was on concept-related stories, that is, stories that use ordinary objects and the immediate environment. Such an approach is a useful way to engage parents in structuring narratives, since it may evoke personal experiences and cultural stories in a less direct way than presenting them with a blank page. An alternative approach might be to encourage stories based on specific topics such as family events or cultural celebrations. In the Brilliant Stories project the initial story-making session occurred without the presence of children, but after the fourth session children and parents worked together on their stories. In these joint sessions, participants worked as a small community, sharing and commenting on each other's stories. To finalise and refine their stories, the parents worked together in pairs and helped each other out. The community facilitators provided several broad 'story sparks', such as a bag full of objects that the parents could ask their children about and use in their stories. The project culminated in the tenth session, where parents and children received Certificates of Achievement and were appointed as Learning Champions. The children received a bag with the logo 'Brilliant Stories' and a printed version of their book. I was invited to this celebration session and witnessed how proud the parents and children were of their self-made stories. The celebration was attended by all the participants as well as community members who were not part of the project but were curious about the stories created by their relatives and friends. There were drinks and snacks and a very joyful atmosphere. The room was dotted with colourful printed pages of participants' stories hung up on pole and panel stands. Some stories were in English; some contained words in different languages. Some of the stories had a fully personal narrative, whereas others were based on random objects shown to parents during the sessions. The participants chatted to each other about their stories and showed them to visitors on the display boards or on the tablets they had on loan for the duration of the project.

A celebration session at the end of a story-making project, in which the participants can share food and chat, is important for community-building and contributes to parents' and children's sense of feeling welcome and part of the community as well as validating their time and expertise. Teachers could stage a celebration in the classroom or as part of a whole-school assembly. Some schools may wish to connect such celebrations to seasonal events, such as Christmas Parents' Assembly and follow specific themes in the stories. For instance, it would be an interesting idea to have parents and children create their own digital books about the ways their families celebrate Christmas.

Overall, Brilliant Stories is a *brilliant* example of harnessing community knowledge and participation to foster positive parent–child experience with digital technologies. The guiding curriculum developed by the Brilliant Stories team is flexible enough to be adapted to other communities and I recommend a detailed look at the team's website.

Examples of online communities and resources for digital story-making

Supporting parents as authors of children's digital books through school or community partnerships is a worthwhile approach to the production of books that are dual-language and that honour children's socio-cultural background. An additional or perhaps in some cases an alternative approach is to connect to existing online communities of parent authors of user-generated dual-language books. Here are some examples of online communities that parents may wish to join.

Unite for Literacy
The Unite for Literacy site can be used for reading dual-language books but also as inspiration for users creating their own stories. The library and approach to authorship may motivate parents/caregivers to create their own digital books. Unite for Literacy was set up to address the challenge of book scarcity among young children (what the founders refer to as 'book deserts' across the world). The website features multimedia and multilingual books, with a large library of digital books with English text and narrations in various minority languages. The pictures in the book are photographs representing diverse children and diverse environments. The books can be used by families who are learning to speak English or by English-speaking families who are learning a different language. The English text is accompanied with a

clear voiceover and simple-to-navigate user interface that displays the book: clicking on the right-facing arrow turns the page and clicking on the loudspeaker icon plays the sound. Different narration languages are available for different titles, with Spanish available for most titles. For example, *Playground* by Holly Hartman is offered in the following languages:

- Arabic (العربية)
- Chinese (中文)
- French (français)
- German (Deutsche)
- Hindi (हिंदी)
- Karen
- Karenni
- Korean (한국어)
- Russian (русский)
- Somali (Soomaali)
- Spanish (español)
- Turkish (Türkçe)
- Vietnamese (Tiếng Việt)

The storylines and overall layout are kept simple and the topic of the narrative realistic and relevant for diverse groups of children. The library is freely available from the project's website:

http://www.uniteforliteracy.com/

Storyweaver

Storyweaver is an inspirational project and platform from a not-for-profit children's book publisher, Pratham Books, that aims to distribute books in multiple Indian languages. The platform started off with a small set of digital books in English and a few Indian languages but has over the past two years grown into a massive online library of digital stories in multiple languages. People's contribution to the bank of stories is actively encouraged by the Storyweaver team and there is an easy-to-use tool to add a digital story to the library. Parents can add translations to existing stories by typing the text directly into the template. The original text is displayed as a guide and, when finished, the translated story can be published on the Storyweaver platform. This is a fantastic way of harnessing the power of community to grow a story bank. Users not only contribute translations but also add their likes and comments to existing stories, thus curating and personalising the database. Some general tips on translation and a step-by-step guide on how to contribute to the story bank are available from this site:

https://storyweaver.org.in/translation_tools_and_tips

In addition to user-generated examples of digital books, there are commercially produced digital books that parents can personalise with their own content. If parents are interested in adding their own voiceover or audio-recording to an existing digital story, then there are two apps that they might find useful.

Me Books

Me Books is an app for iPads and tablets, developed by Made In Me Ltd in the UK. The app is essentially a library of digital books curated by Made In Me; new titles are sent periodically to subscribers. The books are for parents to read with their children. Importantly, parents can personalise them by adding their own voiceover. Thus parents can create their own version of the story, whether it is in their own language or their own interpretation of the text and pictures. They can use the voice-recording to adjust the story's content to the child's understanding and preferences. The voiceover can be co-created by parents and children, with their own music, sounds or parent–child dramatisation of the story. There are no restrictions on fantasy and creativity. Parents and children could jointly consider the voices for different characters and assign to each other roles of narrator and actor.

http://madeinme.com/me-books/

Scene Speak

Scene Speak was developed by Good Karma Applications, Inc., which is a small developer company focusing on apps for children with learning differences, needs and disabilities. Thanks to its versatile and customisable design, this app can be used for diverse purposes, including parents' creation of photo-based digital books. Users can add their own pictures, recordings and even interactive elements to the stories. Unlike other story-making apps, which have a fixed place for adding sound, *Scene Speak* allows you to add spoken words anywhere in the digital book. This means that individual objects in a story can 'speak' and play sounds in selected moments when activated by the reader. A hotspot can also be associated with text labels, enabling a storybook to become part of a vocabulary-teaching exercise. Finished stories can be saved in a digital library, where they can be categorised according to themes. Parents may find the application an attractive space in which they can personalise their children's interactive experiences with digital books and add their own version of the story as well as of its interactive features. The app can be downloaded from the App Store:

https://itunes.apple.com/gb/app/scene-speak/id420492342?mt=8

Chapter summary

Following the premise that parents' involvement in their children's literacy life can be enriching for the entire family, this chapter provided strategies and examples of how parents could author and personalise children's digital books. I have positioned parents as language, literacy and technology brokers and described the key benefits such a role can bring about: validation and valorisation of dual-language/multilingual and multicultural relationships, positive parent–child shared engagement with digital technologies, and joint enjoyment of stories and literacy resources. Parents' digital story-making for and with their young children can be part of families' active involvement in school- or community-mediated informal learning programmes and constitute an essential part of family engagement in children's literacy.

Reflection point

'The Lion' all began with a picture of a faun carrying an umbrella and parcels in a snowy wood. This picture had been in my mind since I was about sixteen. Then one day, when I was about forty, I said to myself, 'Let's try to make a story about it.' (C. S. Lewis)

Every parent will have their own favourite childhood stories. For me it's *Alice's Adventures in Wonderland* and the magical world conjured up by C. S. Lewis. Parents may remember the stories they heard from their parents or grandparents and can use the digital medium to reproduce their own version of classic fairy tales or indigenous stories. It is never too late to be a storyteller or story-maker; we all carry rich fantasies that can be converted into beautiful stories for children. Digital books can be part of the magic that ensues when a child hears or reads a story from the ones they love most. Why not take a classic fairy tale and add your own personal twist to it? Or recount your favourite story to your child and then turn it into a multimedia book?

Further reading

These three books are my favourite titles on the topics of parent involvement, home–school connection and the richness of children's socio-cultural backgrounds:

Brinton, D. M., Kagan, O. & Bauckus, S. (eds) (2017) *Heritage Language Education: A New Field Emerging*. New York: Routledge.

González, N., Moll, L. C. & Amanti, C. (eds) (2006). *Funds of Knowledge: Theorizing Practices in Households, Communities, and Classrooms*. New York: Routledge.

Pahl, K. & Rowsell, J. (2010) *Artifactual Literacies: Every Object Tells a Story*. New York: Teachers College Press.

For more general advice on how to work with families and involve them meaningfully and authentically in school life, see the very useful tips compiled by the Inclusive School Network™ in the section 'Family involvement': https://inclusiveschools.org/category/resources/family-involvement/

This freely available guide to how to read with young children contains some useful strategies that could be adopted for the purpose of sharing digital stories and enjoying family storytime:

Young, R. & Ferguson, P. (2018) 'A guide to reading with young children', Literacy for Pleasure.

https://literacyforpleasure.files.wordpress.com/2018/03/a-guide-to-reading-with-children.pdf

9
Digital libraries and library management systems

This penultimate chapter introduces readers to the increasingly popular world of children's digital libraries and digital library systems. In alignment with the book's focus on agency and reciprocity in personalisation, I give particular attention to the ways in which these systems can position teachers, parents and children as content-makers and co-creators. I divide up the argument and supporting examples into two parts. First, I present the pros and cons of 'static' digital libraries that do not contain data management tools and merely list different books and their availability and location in physical libraries. I suggest that the use of these libraries could involve greater and more direct engagement with children. In the second part, I outline the pros and cons of 'dynamic' digital libraries that can collect and analyse user engagement data. These digital library systems are data driven in that they not only list and store books but also provide information about how users engage with the books, including the duration of reading or teacher–child engagement with specific titles. The user data can be harnessed to offer recommendations or support dialogue around reading in the classroom. I suggest ways in which these data could be harnessed by educational professionals to support community conversations around children's reading. Teachers may be familiar with many of the systems mentioned in this chapter and may be using them for a different purpose in their classrooms. I focus on the purpose of motivating children to read for pleasure, and I emphasise elements relevant to children's agency, adult–child dialogue and communities of readers.

Static digital libraries: advantages and limitations

Digital libraries can help teachers and children find relevant reading content because they can hold unprecedentedly large and diverse assemblages of stories. Besides this availability of titles, the key advantage of digital libraries, compared with physical libraries, is the accessibility. Digital libraries can be accessed by parents, teachers and children anywhere in the world. They are open 24/7 and can offer access to books in various formats. The maintenance and curation of titles do not require as much staff time as in physical libraries. Moreover, digital libraries do not take up any physical space, so are cheaper to run. On the more technical side, digital libraries need regular software updates to provide an easy-to-navigate and attractive user interface. Providers of digital libraries need to make sure that the digital platform is in line with the latest data preservation, management, privacy and security regulations and that they protect not only users' privacy but also the titles they stock against illegal use, copying or distribution. Digital libraries can be extremely beneficial to encouraging resource sharing, exploration and new ways of learning and teaching. There is also the advantage that a digital copy of a digital book can't get lost or damaged as often happens with physical books.

The key disadvantage of digital libraries is that, in their current design, they offer very little space for dialogue about the books and no space for community engagement. Physical libraries are community spaces where people can access the internet, find out about job offers, read magazines and browse books. For children, brick-and-mortar libraries are spaces where they can touch and physically manipulate and browse books they do not have at home. Physical libraries are also important spaces in terms of modelling reading behaviour, since children can see other children and adults engaged in quiet reading. Libraries also offer parents and their young children collective story-related experiences (e.g. storytime sessions facilitated by professional storytellers) and opportunity for parents to meet other parents. Physical libraries have dedicated sections for children's books, whereas digital libraries typically divide up their content according to book characteristics, children's age, reading level and genre. Physical libraries employ librarians who can advise on books' appropriateness and provide recommendations, whereas digital libraries expect teachers or parents to stand in for the absent librarian.

Given their complementary roles, digital and physical libraries should exist side by side. Unfortunately, however, cuts to government funding have led to the reduction or complete removal of libraries in many local communities. Many educators, librarians and community members, including me, have protested against the recent public library closures in the UK. The focus on digital libraries in this chapter is an attempt to raise awareness about their unique role in children's reading but is in no way intended to sideline the important role played by physical libraries. Countries that have developed sustainable systems to maintain physical libraries in their communities have always had my admiration.

Strategies for using static digital libraries

In contemplating strategies to support the use of digital libraries, we can draw some inspiration from teachers' effective use of physical libraries. The common feature is that they model the reading environment, apprentice children into attending the library and guide them in exploring the books it holds. Schools have established routines for connecting to the physical libraries in their communities, with, for example, regular trips organised by individual class teachers. Some schools have very rich collections of books on their premises and involve children in managing book loans and sorting. Some schools have gone the extra mile by creating their own library space, either inside or outside the school building. For example, the UK school of which I am a governor has its own School Library Bus. This is a converted double-decker bus that offers a quiet, fun and comfortable space where children can enjoy books. The bus is parked on the school field and has been renovated with help from local charities.

Of course not all of these inspirational strategies are directly transferable to digital libraries, but similar approaches can be adopted to familiarise children with them. The key difference is that teachers' guidance will need to be accompanied with a digital demonstration of using the library. This could happen either on the interactive whiteboard for the whole class or on children's individual tablets or computers. Teachers can devote some time in their English lessons to showing children the digital books available in digital libraries, click through the navigation path as if guiding children in a physical location and explain how to borrow and return books. Examples of digital libraries that teachers may wish to use with children are included in the next section.

Recommended examples of children's digital libraries

Digital libraries for schools are typically based on whole-school subscription models but there are also some that are freely available. Teachers may consider the possibility of children accessing a digital library from home and encourage them to choose titles for themselves. Just like planning visits to physical libraries, teachers can plan children's 'visits' online to explore digital libraries. For example, they can allocate some time at the end of an English lesson for children to browse the latest titles or renew their book loans. The key message to convey to children is that digital libraries provide legitimate spaces to nurture their interest to read and that digital books can be an integral part of their reading diet.

The International Children's Digital Library

My primary example of a recommended digital library is the ICDL, which offers free access to high-quality digital books from around the world:
http://en.childrenslibrary.org/

The ICDL was established in November 2002 and caters for children aged between three and thirteen. In 2018, it lists 4,619 books in 59 languages. The ICDL's mission is to promote reading but also the cultural value of books. This mission is underscored by the fact that the ICDL offers e-books in 15 different languages from 27 cultures. The library was designed in partnership with a research team led by Allison Druin from the University of Maryland, which adopted a unique approach to the design of the digital user interface. Druin's (2005) team collaborated with children in designing the ICDL and pioneered the direct involvement of children in the design of technology-based environments. The library's success is thus a testament to what can be achieved through co-design with children. Researchers at the University of Maryland have published several academic papers (e.g. Druin et al. 2003) that describe the benefits of child-mediated design and their approach has become prominent in the field of computer design. The children's involvement has meant that the library does not contain typical genre-led categories of books. Professor Druin's research shows that children use different criteria when searching for books. When developing the library search categories for children *with* children, the researchers noticed that adult categories of fiction and non-fiction made little sense to young readers. Instead, the children suggested categories such as 'happy' or 'scary' books or books with spiders and princesses. The CDL can be accessed via the web browser on any device; as far as I know, most schools access it on desktop computers. For iPads, the library can be accessed as a free iOS app:
https://itunes.apple.com/gb/app/icdl-free-books-for-children-international-childrens/id363731638?mt=8

Oxford Owl

Another large collection of digital books is the Oxford Owl library run by Oxford University Press. Oxford Owl is a paid subscription library for

UK schools, but it also offers a free e-book library with a collection of selected Oxford Owl titles. The site is for three- to eleven-year-olds and offers about 200 titles categorised according to age, reading level, book type and Oxford Owl series (Project X, ReadWriteInc., Biff, Chip and Kipper adventures, etc.). The digital books have limited interactivity but are likely to engage children because of their attractive illustrations and professionally recorded voiceovers. The library can be accessed from the publisher's website:

https://www.oxfordowl.co.uk/for-home/find-a-book/library-page

StoryPlace

StoryPlace is a free book depository for computer-based digital books. Users need to have Adobe Flash installed to access all its titles. The digital library carries titles for pre-schoolers only. The 'Book Hive' offers several stories, and the 'Preschool Activity Library' offers matched activities for each story. The site is available in English and Spanish:

https://www.storyplace.org/

Nalibali

In addition to digital databases of stories in English, teachers can introduce children to digital libraries with books in different languages. For example, Nalibali offers titles in African languages and English. Nalibali was developed and is curated as part of the Project for the Study of Alternative Education in South Africa (PRAESA). PRAESA is an independent research and development unit affiliated with the University of Cape Town, which seeks to support children's love of reading with titles in local languages. It offers digital books that can be printed out or read online. Besides English, Nalibali titles are available in 10 African languages: Afrikaans, Sepedi, Sesotho, Setswana, Siswati, Tshivenda, Xitsonga, isiNdebele, isiXhosa and isiZulu

http://nalibali.mobi/stories

TumbleBooks

TumbleBooks is a popular digital library site in Canada with interactive audio picturebooks for children of pre-school and lower primary-school age. TumbleBooks can be presented to children as a digital library they can access from home with their parents. It is a subscription site with books based on popular picturebooks with added audio (narration and music) and some basic animation. Children can listen to the story or interact with it with the narration switched off. They can access the books on any reading device (if you're using a tablet go to the TumbleMobile site) and teachers who subscribe to the site can access lesson plans in alignment with Canada's Common Core.

http://asp.tumblebooks.com/Default.aspx

Wheelers Books

Wheelers Books prides itself to be the largest supplier of digital books in Australasia, with a huge database of 20.2 million titles. The platform is advertised to teachers and librarians who might wish to license specific titles. For teachers working with international communities of readers, it is worth having a look at the content diversity enabled by its massive database.

https://www.wheelersbooks.com.au/info/ebooks

Literature for Children

Literature for Children is an example par excellence of how digital books can enrich traditional libraries. The site shows that, whereas physical copies of the same titles would be difficult to make freely available en masse, digital copies can be shared, saved as a digital copy or printed out as a PDF. The site offers 74 free digital books that can be read via an internet browser. The unique feature of the site is that it features copyright-free books published in the United States and Great Britain between 1850 and 1923. The digitisation of these titles was funded through the US National Endowment for the Humanities and the site is hosted by the University of Florida. Most of the titles are from the Baldwin Library of Historical Children's Literature, housed in the Department of Special Collections and Area Studies at the University of Florida. Despite the age of the titles, their digital display presents scanned pages with vivid colours. This digital library is an important example of how digital libraries can enrich reading: rather than focusing on bestsellers and currently popular titles, they can play an important role in reviving classic stories and historic illustrations.

http://palmm.digital.flvc.org/islandora/search/?type=edismax &collection=palmm%3Ajuv

BorrowBox

BorrowBox is not a digital library (book depository) per se but rather a digital intermediate between an existing library collection and a school's access to it. *BorrowBox* can be installed on any digital device. Once installed, it enables users to download digital books in a format compatible with their device. Users need to be registered with a local library to be able to download selected digital books. They can also search, browse and request loans. Books are arranged by age, genre, author, series and for audio-books also by narrator. Unique features include recommendations of similar titles and the facility to read and listen to book previews. Some libraries offer their own curated lists of titles. Given a connection to a local library, users can make instant loans or reservations of physical books as well. If a digital book is accessed through the app, *BorrowBox* saves where the reader has stopped and offers a digital bookmark. *BorrowBox* works as an app for Apple devices:

https://itunes.apple.com/gb/app/borrowbox-library/id5628 43562?mt=8

– or Android devices:

https://play.google.com/store/apps/details?id=com.bolindadigital.BorrowBoxLibrary&hl=en_GB

Dynamic digital libraries: key advantages and limitations

Library management systems, sometimes referred to as 'digital reading systems' or 'dynamic digital libraries', are digital collections of children's books that act not only as book-holding sites but also as data management sites. These systems can help teachers and children find relevant content, archive readers' responses to individual titles, collect and manage data on users' activity and share such data with relevant parties. Unlike static digital libraries, dynamic digital libraries contain data management tools that can provide tailored recommendations of new titles based on readers' engagement with the database and their selection of genres and difficulty levels. Some data management systems integrate tools such as social media and the option to share favourite titles with one's followers. Dynamic digital libraries that are offered to schools can also produce data analytics and descriptive data analyses, which teachers can use to evaluate and develop their mentoring practice with specific children. For example, the systems can generate an at-a-glance-view of which books have been accessed, requested or returned by individual children. Teachers can request data and statistical comparisons of children's engagement with the database and can curate the database by adding/removing titles and categorising them according to the abilities of the children in their classes.

Some classroom-based research shows that dynamic digital libraries can enhance classroom provision and motivate children to read more (Picton & Clark 2015), especially if they are initially reluctant to read print books, which is often the case for young boys (Picton 2014). The key advantage of dynamic digital libraries is that they position reading as a recreational and enjoyable activity rather than just a technical or functional skill. This is important because the international drive towards testing in schools often degrades reading to a functional skill and non-leisure activity. Another asset of dynamic digital libraries is that they can individualise book or author recommendations and keep track of individual children's engagement – a level of personalisation that a teacher in a typically sized class will not have time to do. Last but not least, the systems address professional and practical constraints, since they hold thousands of book titles that children can access, which would not be possible with a traditional library (unless a school joins an external library).

Thanks to the data management tools, dynamic digital libraries can recommend titles by drawing on a huge database and match information about books with children's preferences. For example, if users click on a book recommended by the RM Books Depository (http://www.browns-bfs.co.uk/vlebooks/vle-primary), the system registers this book on the user's virtual bookshelf. Through a management dashboard, the teacher can access the bookshelves of all students and see which books were read and for how long. In addition, users can comment on each other's titles, exchange comments about books they like to read and even access information about their favourite authors, all in one virtual space.

There are some limitations to dynamic digital libraries. Teresa Cremin and I have argued (Kucirkova & Cremin 2017) that the design of the most popular digital library systems does not align with socio-cultural theories of learning. We looked at the key features of some popular digital libraries and compared them with theories of learning. We found that current digital reading systems address some immediate practical challenges faced by teachers in the classroom and therefore have significant practical value. However, the systems position teachers in restrictive and restricted roles as librarians, curators and monitors rather than as mentors, listeners and co-readers. Professor Cremin and I suggest that, instead of as curators, dynamic digital libraries could position teachers as co-readers who can model and contextualise reading behaviour in the classroom (e.g. by giving teachers an attractive space to share their own favourite titles and reading preferences and practices). Instead of acting in the capacity of an absent librarian, teachers could be positioned as listeners. These roles relate to the notion of agency and reciprocity. Our article encourages designers to rethink the way they approach digital reading spaces for children. However, it is worth remembering that even bad design can be transformed into a new experience. We encourage teachers to co-create the online reading space and enhance its personalisation features through community-oriented dialogue around books. For example, teachers can share their own reading habits by creating digital reading diaries and marking specific book titles on the platform. They can also invite children into dialogue about books by sharing their own choices of specific titles that children may browse on the platform or borrow.

Teachers play a central role in how the existing systems are used (or not used). My recommended strategies for the use of dynamic digital libraries focus on two issues: appropriate use of children's data and the enhancement of classroom dialogue.

Strategies for using dynamic digital libraries

The use of children's data to enhance their reading experiences is a new way of encouraging reading for pleasure in the digital age. There is no blueprint or evidence-based way of how to do this well. In what follows, I draw on some of my experiences with the systems, and some broader ideas from research on effective pedagogy, to make suggestions how teachers may engage positively with digital library systems to facilitate learning benefits for children.

The safety and security of children's data

First and foremost, it is essential that children's data collected through the systems are kept safe and secure. In order to provide children with recommendations, digital libraries need to collect information about individual children's likes and history of reading. This information is typically supplied to the systems by the teacher or by the children, who fill out a short questionnaire about their reading preferences. Information about reading habits can also be provided to the system less directly when the library monitors children's use of the library. Based on the patterns of behaviour, the library derives children's level of reading and interest in specific titles. It is essential that teachers and children are fully aware of the data collection and monitoring purposes of the digital libraries they use. Children's data are analysed by algorithms, and algorithms are not neutral tools: they are typically designed with commercial, not only educational, intentions. Information about children's engagement with digital books is typically stored in the cloud, so the providers of digital libraries need to guarantee that children's data are stored securely and not sold for marketing purposes. If schools keep children's data, they need to make sure they have valid reasons for storing them. They should not keep children's data just for the sake of archiving them; they should securely dispose of any data they no longer need for assessment purposes.

The use and misuse of personal data by large companies have featured in public discourse (e.g. the Cambridge Analytica scandal) and media headlines. Digital libraries are not immune to potential data breaches and misuse of data by external companies. Teachers who use digital library systems in the classroom therefore need to ensure that children's data are protected and that the systems' providers comply with regulations on data access, encryption and retention. On many platforms, children can share their own stories, book ratings, preferences, reading progress logs and even videos. In the UK and mainland Europe, the General Data Protection Regulation (GDPR) applies to all organisations that handle personal data. GDPR is a pan-European regulation that applies to small and big organisations, including children's app designers and book publishers.

Although the responsibility for handling children's data lies with the providers of digital libraries, data interpretation is carried out by individual teachers. It is important to remember in this process that digital reading logs do not represent children's *entire* reading engagement (e.g. the system will not log what children read at home or on their way to school at the bus stop) and that behind each data point lies a complex reading pattern.

Enhancing dialogue through dynamic digital libraries

A promising element of dynamic digital libraries relates to the online dialogue spaces that they create. The commenting features and possibilities for children to leave feedback on specific titles are likely to encourage children's engagement with the platform and conversations with their peers. Moreover, some dynamic digital libraries run a news feed or chat on their platform and some even host reading forums. These features add novelty and opportunities for synchronous conversations.

Teachers are unlikely to have the time to monitor an online chat, but they can direct discussion through strategically suggesting discussion topics. For instance, teachers could frame students' online conversations on a platform with regular requests for them to review new books and share their views on what they liked or disliked about the books. For example, students could be asked to write a review of John Green's *The Fault in Our Stars*, displaying their own comments next to the book and other students' feedback. Teachers could also set up community contests, ask the children to rate their favourite titles and announce the class's favourite title each week. The more that teachers can introduce a shared element that brings the class together as a community of readers, the more likely the platform will be used by children in a dialogic way in which each child's reader identity is valued.

Different digital library systems have different characteristics and functionalities, so their use needs to be informed by the instructions provided by the individual systems. By way of illustration, I have selected some examples of digital library and digital reading management systems and shall describe their key features. I have seen most of these systems in use in schools, but some descriptions are based on the provider's description, so caution should be exercised in interpreting the systems' capabilities.

Examples of children's digital libraries

MLS Books

The Micro Librarian System (MLS) offers a suite of associated products, including the Reading Cloud (see below). The titles in MLS have been chosen in collaboration with librarians and Peters Educational Books, which pride themselves on being 'the best children's library supplier in the country'. The collection features predominantly UK authors and topics relevant to the UK primary curriculum, with more than 1,100 titles for primary school and 1,500 titles for secondary schools. Digital books offered through MLS Books can be read on any device, including PCs and tablets, which is a major advantage for schools. Schools that subscribe to the system can monitor the usage of individual titles by individual children. Subscribers can also build their own library collection customised for groups of students and select from a database (called OverDrive) of more than 500,000 digital books and audio-books.

MLS Reading Cloud

The MLS Reading Cloud is the reading system part of MLS and offers a digital reading community, with conversation-supporting features such as opportunities to access featured authors and most popular books and to comment on and share individual titles. Children can add their blogs and write or even video-record their own book reviews. They can chat in the Reading Cloud secure system with other students about their favourite books or authors and add their 'likes' and recommendations of titles, as on a social media system. Children have access to the digital school library via the Reading Cloud, so they can search and download titles and share what they read (i.e. their personal library) with other users. MLS regularly updates the site with book-related news and words and facts of the day.

https://www.readingcloud.net/

RM Books

RM Books is similar to MLS in that it features both a digital library and a reading management system and is based on a subscription model available to UK schools. The system has been tested and evaluated in schools in partnership with the National Literacy Trust in a study in 2014/15. Picton and Clark (2015) concluded that use of the system motivated children to read and was a useful tool for teachers to monitor children's reading habits. The RM digital library features titles from popular publishers such as Penguin Random House and each book can be annotated with digital notes. These notes can be text based or can take the form of short audio or video clips.

Another feature of the reading management system is the customisation option to create small libraries for groups of children or individual children. Teachers can allocate books to such mini-libraries using the system's guide to reading levels and key topics. In the teachers' dashboard, they can then track how long and how much the students have read particular books and even see which page was read last by an individual student. The subscribing school does not own the digital titles but rather rents them for a fixed period of time. Rental periods are per student or groups of students and can be a week, month, term or year. The system works on PCs as well as tablets and can be usefully employed in both school and home-learning environments.

Epic!

Epic! is a subscription system popular in US schools as well as homes. The platform offers access to some 25,000 e-book titles, most of which are a combination of text and illustrations. The site is specifically designed for home and school use with a neat user interface. The library can be accessed on any device. The large number of titles available through the library will be attractive to teachers seeking to engage children with content they may not have come across before. The books are offered in three age categories: under fives, six to eight years, and nine to twelve years. The subscription model gives access to e-books and also interactive quizzes and videos.

https://www.getepic.com/

Padlet

Given that not many freely available digital libraries contain space to discuss stories, teachers can use existing collaborative tools to invite contributions from children as well as their parents. Padlet is an easy-to-use tool that can be used to profile teachers' reader identities and encourage communication about children's story authorship. This tool is suitable for older children or for children who can use it with their parents. No signup is required and collaborations are potentially unlimited. Teachers can choose who they invite to the shared digital board and can assign to individual collaborators the roles of writer and moderator. There are multiple ways of sharing content and commenting on it, which offer great possibilities for dialogue around stories.

https://en-gb.padlet.com/

Chapter summary

This chapter has established that digital libraries can usefully complement physical libraries by providing access to large databases of books and tailored recommendations based on children's engagement with what they read. Teachers can enlarge the classroom's or school's book provision by providing access to online book depositories such as the ICDL. Teachers should be aware of the potential of dynamic digital library systems to encourage dialogue around books and to use children's data to provide targeted recommendations. All digital library systems need to comply with best practice in personal data management and storage. Teachers can harness the opportunities for expanded reading that these systems offer and thereby strengthen the reading community in their classrooms and beyond.

Reflection point

No two persons ever read the same book. (Edmund Wilson)

This quote always reminds me of the many ways in which books can be interpreted and internalised and of the importance of dialogue around books. Facilities to store and share digital books online offer multiple access points to a wider range of contents than was previously accessible. They also provide opportunities for rich dialogue about books. Digital libraries could become sites in which to capture and nurture such dialogue. Perhaps the key role for twenty-first-century teachers of reading for pleasure is to encourage this kind of participatory dialogue with children early on in their education. What do you think?

Further reading

These three books do not address digital library systems per se, but they cover in depth the importance of dialogue and community-building around literacy and technologies in the classroom. They are authored by leading experts in literacy and technology. If you can't access these specific titles, I recommend you look up other books by Henrietta Dombey, Teresa Cremin, Neil Mercer, Karen Littleton and John Potter.

Bearne, E., Dombey, H. & Grainger, T. (2003) *Classroom Interactions in Literacy*. Maidenhead: McGraw-Hill.

Mercer, N. & Littleton, K. (2007) *Dialogue and the Development of Children's Thinking: A Sociocultural Approach*. London: Routledge.

Turvey, K., Potter, J., Burton, J., Allen, J. & Sharp, J. (2016) *Primary Computing and Digital Technologies: Knowledge, Understanding and Practice*. London: SAGE.

For readers interested in how digital libraries handle personal data, I recommend this white paper co-authored with the HAT (Hub-of-All-Things) Community. It describes the data challenges and possibilities as well as the technical requirements of educational systems handling children's data. It is freely available from the UCL Document Depository page:
http://discovery.ucl.ac.uk/1568437/

10

Innovative approaches to support personalised multimedia story-making

Like 'Tomorrow's World' L&L!

This final chapter introduces you to a story territory that is currently uncharted by state schools: the interconnection between physical objects and virtual story worlds. Whereas in everyday life we frequently use digital objects that are connected to virtual spaces through RFID (radio-frequency identification) technology (e.g. when swiping a credit card at the entrance to an underground station), this technology has not yet entered public educational systems.

This chapter aims to introduce educational professionals to the potential of this and related technologies, notably their potential to support children's reader identities and agency in learning. Children's personal stories can be scaffolded with physical objects that are connected to multimedia files with RFID technology or wirelessly. Such digital systems are already embedded in many popular children's games, which indicates the need for teachers to be aware of these technologies' potentials and limitations. In addition to technologies that connect the digital and physical, I shall describe some organisations that connect classroom-based and virtual stories through story museums and galleries. To end the chapter, I return to the line of argument in the previous chapters and discuss the community and agentic aspect of children's reading on screen. I conclude with some inspiring examples of digital communities that welcome story authorship and conversation.

Innovation in educational technologies: what do teachers think?

One big caveat has to be made: this chapter focuses on pioneering ideas and innovative educational technologies, but innovation in industry and the commercial sector does not always equate to progress in educational terms. Launching a product may guarantee it will be the first product on the market but not a long-term (or even in some cases short-term) learning benefit for children. Whereas some companies operate according to a trial and error model, educationalists stand on a foundation provided by previous researchers and professionals. Therefore, many educational technology researchers, including me (e.g. Kucirkova 2017d), have advocated interdisciplinary and industry–research models where knowledge and skills work together to innovate in the educational sector. Collaborative industry–research models are not the norm; their instantiation entails the allocation of resources and also changes in attitudes towards what constitutes research and business success. Innovation in educational technologies should be received with a cautious open mind by all three stakeholders: researchers, teachers and designers.

Researchers, teachers and designers innovating together

Traditional educational research has historically been concerned with documenting and evaluating what was rather than what could be. Conversely, successful technology companies have relied on models that test the technology with a small group of children but sell it to large groups. Teachers are caught in-between the research and industry efforts and get little say about how research or design could be improved. Yet, teachers could play a crucial role in research–industry collaborations. Teachers have a unique position in mediating not only children's access to technologies in the classroom but also children's use of technology at home. The latter is accomplished through parent evenings, teachers' conversations with parents and school newsletters and messaging dedicated to technology use. For example, many schools in the UK have a dedicated ICT safety section on their website where they advise parents on appropriate controls and settings. Teachers' knowledge of children's learning is uniquely contextualised by children's everyday lives, and teachers' insights can therefore yield new perspectives relevant to both researchers and designers/developers. While the industry is churning out more powerful and sophisticated tools, researchers are still looking for definitions. Given the uneven pace of industry production and research dissemination, it is often individual teachers' attitudes and technological savviness that determine whether children will or will not have access to the latest technology trends.

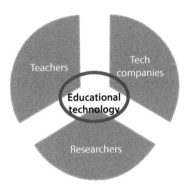

Figure 10.1   Teachers, tech companies and researchers working together to innovate and progress technologies for children.
Source: Author

It is imperative that the three different stakeholder groups – teachers, designers and researchers – work together on the development of educational technologies. Certainly, each stakeholder group has their own agenda but the trio share responsibility for children's wellbeing. This shared commitment is depicted in Figure 10.1.

In general, the discussion of benefits and limitations of educational technology should be cognisant of the three-way influence of innovation, evaluation and application practices represented by developers, teachers and researchers. The question of whether we consider innovation in the children's toy industry to be design inventiveness or commercial exploitation would require another and longer discussion. My aim is to ensure that teachers have at least some awareness of how the mechanisms in smart learning environments work.

Smart learning environments

School version of the internet of things

Tangibles, the internet of toys (IoT) and intelligent objects are part of the smart learning trends that are increasingly being adopted by toy and digital games companies in Western countries. Smart learning environments are personalised, data driven and part of 'today's innovation-rich, networked, cloud-based and data-driven learning environments' (Hoel & Mason 2018, p. 1). I am limiting my description of smart learning environments to the aspects that are most directly linked to this book's focus on reading on screen: tangibles and smart technologies that connect physical objects to digital fictional stories.

Tangibles

Tangibles – aka 'tangible computing systems', 'tangible user interfaces' or 'phygital objects' – can be thought of as systems that connect physical objects (artefacts) and digital platforms. Given this connection between the digital and physical, they have considerable potential for young children's learning. There are various ways in which physical objects can be connected to digital platforms such as digital libraries or video games. The most popular and functional way is the RFID system.

The RFID tagging system consists of a small chip that connects to a digital system through a small antenna. The chip can be tiny (so tiny that it can be implanted under the skin of a finger) but, to function, it requires a reader, that is, a technology that enables the connection between the chip and the digital system. Such a reader can be provided with a smartphone. For example, travellers now frequently pay for public travel by scanning their phone or in restaurants by scanning their debit card to make a contactless payment. The connecting technology used here does not require internet connection, which is an important practical asset for spaces such as underground stations or for tagging animals who move around without a stable internet connection.

RFID technology is being increasingly leveraged by toy manufacturers. Instead of connecting the chip to process a payment, the technology can be used to unlock a feature in a game or to progress a digital story. Commercial uses include popular children's toy sets and video games such as *Skylanders*, *Pokemon Ramble* or *Disney Infinity Toys*. These toys work on the principle of so-called decentralised RFID tagging, which involves multiple copies of the same artefact to connect to a specific point in a video game. For example, with *Skylanders*, parents can buy for their children *Skylanders* figures that appear to be non-digital, but as soon as they are placed on the reader they activate a specific virtual functionality. The reader is a special pad that connects to the game on the screen: it reads the tag and activates a specific sequence in the digital game. Each *Skylanders* figure carries a tag that unlocks its virtual version (avatar) in the game.

The teachers I interviewed as part of my Economic and Social Research Council (ESRC) project on personalised stories were not aware of RFID or of figures connected to digital games. Yet, in the very classroom where I held the interviews I noticed many children keeping their *Skylanders* figures in their 'home trays' (trays in which children keep their personal belongings in this school). The use of RFID technology for story-related games is a significant motivational factor for children.

These toys are not cheap and represent for many children a status symbol. Children like to bring their *Skylanders* figures to school or carry them to their friend's house to activate their own part in a shared game. What I always highlight to the teachers is the fact that the connection between the physical toy and the digital game is determined by the commercial producer, not by a teacher or the child. The commercial providers develop the toys and the technology that reads the tags incorporated in these toys and the games the children play. These toy manufacturers thus influence two markets and two environments in one go: the physical world of toys and the virtual world of games. Now let's imagine that part of the equation is influenced by another group of stakeholders: parents, teachers, librarians and the children themselves. Let's imagine that users themselves decide which objects get connected to which digital stories. There is no need to buy these objects and the stories are not driven by monetised mechanisms but are based on the users' own stories, agendas and fantasies. This is the approach followed in some recent research-led projects aligned with the agency/reciprocity framework.

Strategies for using tangibles to enrich children's digital stories

Stories2Connect

In the research project Stories2Connect, led by Candice Satchwell at the University of Central Lancashire, a collection of artefacts were co-designed by the project participants to share with a range of audiences. The project's aim was to use the latest technology to share children's and young people's stories of resilience. The project was nested in a participatory model to conduct research with disadvantaged young people, who are positioned as experts on their lives and authors of their own stories. The project involved, inter alia, the development of an interactive picture map, a suitcase of stories and an Arcade Machine that displayed children's digital stories within the artefact of a tangible game machine. The stories were recorded as video files. Users could access and manipulate them with, for example, the joysticks and buttons of the Arcade Machine. The technology used was a Raspberry Pi computer that connected the video files to the tangible interface. The benefits of such representations of children's stories are not necessarily quantifiable but have been significant for the participants' lives. Dr Satchwell wrote that 'Through their participation in the project the children become powerful as not only providers of stories, but tellers of them'. There was keen public interest in the participants' personal stories, and the various artefacts were displayed in several public areas where community members could listen to and 'play' children's stories. Crucially, the children and young people were positioned as those who decided and led the ways in which their stories were shared. The children were instrumental in the representation of their stories on screen as films and also off screen as books, and even in the connection between the two. More about Stories2Connect is available from the project website:

> http://stories2connect.org/

The Magic Cloud

The importance of children's authorship and agency was also the driving force in our project with the Magic Cloud technology. Magic Cloud was developed by PlingToys Ltd and has an open-ended design with no pre-established connection between tags and digital content. Magic Cloud connects tangible artefacts to digital files through a simple tagging system: a RFID reader is placed inside a cushion in the shape of a cloud and a set of tags are supplied with the kit, which can be placed on any physical object that fits the size of the cushion. The tag can be linked to any digital file that the teacher uploads to the computer and links the object with. For example, teachers can link a natural object, such as a pebble, with an audio file of a rain song. In our project with a local school, we explored how Magic Cloud could be used to motivate children to read for pleasure by connecting their favourite objects to existing digital stories. Teachers shared with us several ideas for how the system could connect classroom objects to audio-recorded stories or curriculum-related activities. The teachers' and children's enthusiasm in exploring Magic Cloud encouraged us to develop the technology further. Magic Cloud can be ordered from PlingToys Ltd:

> http://www.magiccloud.co.uk/

Smart toys and the internet of toys

Another important technology that is part of children's smart learning environments at home and in some pre-schools and schools is the IoT, also known as 'toys that listen' or 'smart toys'; these are character toys that have digital dimensions and connections (Ihamäki & Heljakka 2017). You can think of these toys as physical objects that are connected to the internet, through which they are granted some additional functionalities.

An example of a popular smart toy, which is advertised as educational for young children and linked to stories, is Dino by CogniToys (https://cognitoys.com/). This smart toy can tell jokes, play songs, games and riddles and teach children some basic mathematical concepts. In terms of story-related features, Dino can 'tell a story' (that is, it can select one of the preloaded audio files stored by the system). It can also repeat what the child has said and define a word. Children can personalise the toy by giving it their own name and attuning the toy to their voice. As with other internet-connected things, the more that the child uses it, the better the toy becomes at producing appropriate answers and the more personal, interesting and motivational it becomes for the child.

Smart toys like Dino work on the same technological principle as the voice-recognition personal assistants widely used in households and in smartphones. Each technology giant has their own version: iPhone has Siri, Android (Google devices) has Google Now, Amazon has Alexa and Windows 10's assistant is called Cortana. These virtual personal assistants respond to simple questions and commands. For example, they can answer questions such as 'What's the weather like in London now?' or they can order a pizza delivery and create shopping lists. When connected to home devices, personal assistants can also control light settings in your home. The key difference between home and smartphone personal assistants is that whereas, say, Amazon Echo (home assistant) is stationary, Siri is as portable as the smartphone in which it is embedded. While Alexa uses the Bing search engine, Google assistants use the Google search engine. At the time of writing, neither of the two systems is yet fully developed and users regularly report technical glitches. Although home assistants are not advertised for children, it is important that teachers are aware of these technologies, for two reasons. First, the working principle behind these technologies follows the same logic as that in the design of children's IoT: to execute commands and deliver information. Typical tasks for the home assistant Google Home are to play favourite music from a list of stored tracks, get the latest news from a radio station or inform users about the latest weather forecast. Second, home assistants are available in a child's home, and so it is very likely that children see them in use or even use them with their adult relatives. As such, they are part of children's everyday experience at home.

It is also important to note that the technical glitches in adult smart technologies are not dissimilar from the scandals associated with children's smart toys. It is good for teachers to be aware of them. The most prominent cases relating to smart toys were two high-profile hacking cases of Hello Barbie and VTech in 2015. The cases showed how easily these toys could be hacked and the data they collected about users could be exposed. The smart toy Hello Barbie was found to pose significant data security and privacy threats, and concerns were raised about the commercial nature of the data the toy collects about young children. In particular, Hello Barbie audio-records what children tell the doll and adults can access this audio-recording and share it on social media. Such functionalities raise important ethical questions about the nature of children's play and about the privacy of children's personal stories. The recordings made by an interactive toy are stored by its producer and can be listened back to by anyone who has access to them (and at times by unauthorised users).

Smart toys can only interact with their users if they are connected to the internet and the connection to the internet is not always secure. Moreover, companies producing IoT products have not, at least in the early stages of their production, followed the rules on data security and data protection. This is why Taylor and Michael (2016) labelled smart toys 'the stuff of nightmares' and many researchers, including me, have advocated that all smart toys producers follow codes for the protection of children's data, such as GDPR in the UK and European Union and the Children's Online Privacy Protection Act (COPPA) in the US, and that national governments enforce the laws and defend the interests of children, not industry.

With increasingly more devices and educational resources produced with algorithmic and 'smart' affordances, it is likely that IoT will become more prevalent among young children, requiring an increase in teachers' input and mediation. Despite many educators' legitimate concerns, the reality is that smart toys continue to be produced and to be used by young children and that in many households children interact with household assistants such as Amazon Echo. Although young children are often unaware that the toys are recording them, they understand that they can give these toys commands and expect an answer from them. Smart toys' availability and popularity among young children justify the need for teachers' involvement in mediating children's interaction with them. Moreover, smart toys have the advantage of motivating children to take part in certain activities, and it will be important to ensure that these activities are educationally sound. In light of these pragmatic considerations and my firm belief that the future of educational technology should be shaped by educational professionals, I include some strategies for using smart toys in schools.

Strategies for using smart toys to enrich children's digital stories

I have not come across any independent research that involves teachers' use of smart toys in schools. In the case of such a novel technology, the teacher may be positioned as a researcher who is exploring the usefulness of the technology together with the children. My suggested strategies are therefore common-sense strategies based on the principles of ethical social research with children.

One of the first key measures that teachers (and parents and other adults interested in using smart toys with children) will need to evaluate is whether recordings of children's voices are stored by the provider and if so where. If children's interactions with the smart toys are stored on the provider's servers, the provider needs to ensure their protection. For smart toys used in the UK and Europe, there should be a clear and concise statement about the manufacturer's commitment to GDPR.

It is also important that teachers check whether children's audio-recordings can be shared and if so whether the sharing mechanism requires an adult's input. There should be password-protected access to sharing mechanisms such as the activation of access to social media. Given that many young children are unaware of the fact that they are being recorded by the toy they play with, it is also important that teachers explain to children that their conversations with the toy are not fully private. The best way to explain this to young children is to show them, step by step, how the toy works. Teachers can audio-record the child's voice and then play it back to them. They need to show children the individual buttons and explain how the recording works. Children's ongoing consent and understanding about being recorded in this way should be sought throughout their interaction with the toy. Teachers who decide to mediate children's use of smart toys in the classroom will also need to monitor how the children's relationship with the toy affects their relationships with their friends and other, non-digital, toys. This again is best mediated through conversation, perhaps in a small-group setting where children can ask questions and try out the technology.

Community digital/physical projects

The connection between digital stories and physical objects does not need to be digitally mediated: it can also be embedded in a community of people. This principle is at the heart of various community projects that connect personal stories with artefacts (mostly photographs and personal objects) and bring together digital technologies and communities of readers and storytellers. Such projects can foster intergenerational dialogue, multi-organisational collaboration and story-mediated models of conversation. Given the community orientation of these projects, they are closely aligned with the agency/reciprocity framework. I shall describe the ways in which they were carried out in hopes of inspiring some strategies of your own.

Rachel Heydon, from Western University in Canada, is a key scholar of intergenerational literature, with a fascinating profile of projects that document and manifest the connections between intergenerational traditions and technological innovations. Dr Heydon experienced the benefits of growing up in an intergenerational family and has conducted several studies that show the positive influence of intergenerational dialogue upon children as well as the elderly. The focus in Heydon's work is particularly on intergenerational centres in Canada, in which young children and elderly community members interact and learn from each other. In 2005, Heydon showed how the joint creation of picture-based books and booklets with personal story content positively shaped feelings of belonging and identity for both children and the elderly. In 2007, Heydon documented how children and adults' co-creation of visual artefacts such as drawings and artwork contributed to increased communication among them. The projects took place in intergenerational children's centres in Canada, which are daycare centres for children where multiple generations (parents, grandparents, aunties, uncles, elders) interact with and learn from each other. Although the intergenerational centres are primarily geared towards Aboriginal families, bringing families back together is sorely needed in almost all urban communities. Stories are a wonderful intergenerational glue that can be brought into use with technology, as illustrated in Heydon and colleagues' projects.

Similar findings were obtained in one of my intergenerational projects with Karen Littleton, in which we explored the usefulness of digital story-making with children in a local school and with elderly community members. In Kucirkova (2016a) I describe the 'Remember' Community Project, in which a team of researchers from the Open University partnered up with two technology companies (AirWatch and Aerohive), a local parish network and two Year 4 classrooms in a local lower school to creatively explore intergenerational technology-mediated collaboration. The theme guiding the project was Remembrance, which is an important part of British life and the school curriculum. The school designed activities that would link the topic to History, English and Citizenship curriculum areas and welcomed the opportunity to combine a multi-media approach with efforts to remember and honour victims and survivors of the world wars.

Over the course of six months, the participating children collected personal stories about the Second World War from elderly members of the community who had volunteered to participate in the project. These volunteers were recruited through the local community organisation Love Woburn Sands and their visit to the school was facilitated through the organisation's leader. The volunteers talked to the children about their memories of the war, which the children audio-recorded and made notes about. The children then used the *Our Story* app to make multimedia stories about individuals' memories of the war. They used pictures from the internet to accompany the stories and excerpts from voice-recordings of the elderly sharing their experiences. For example, children took a photograph of a banana and inserted it into a story page that described the lack of fruit during wartime, as recounted by one of the elderly visitors. Overall, the project contributed to a deeper understanding of technology-mediated education and community relationships but also provided distinct benefits for the individual project partners: the technology companies facilitated secure and efficient storage and transfer of personal digital content; the school innovated its practice through participation in a research-informed approach to digitally mediated learning; the local parish network benefited from enhanced community engagement with the wider public and older generations. For the teachers, the project yielded a large amount of new information around creative exploration of traditional themes (Remembrance) and ways in which teachers can enrich extant teaching resources with digital materials and foster intergenerational dialogue in a local community.

There are some inspirational examples of online platforms that facilitate story exchanges on a daily basis and within international communities. Visiting the sites and exploring the stories they feature may help teachers contextualise these ideas in their own classroom. These platforms can be described as digital book-related platforms that offer the possibility for users to upload their own content. They act as sites of convergence, or 'hubs', that not only collate digital stories but also encourage their creation, valuation and distribution. I have selected a few that I have come across in my work with teachers and children in the UK.

Digital story hubs for children

The PopUpHub

The PopUpHub funded by the Paul Hamlyn Foundation is a UK site dedicated to creating and sharing digital stories. The site is designed in the style of a story-making factory, with an Engine Room, Factory, Showroom and Control Centre areas. In the Engine Room, users can search for books using the following search criteria: book title, book's author, UK school that participates in PopUpHub, UK region (where the participating schools are based) and children's age range. If you select a specific school, you will be directed to this school's review of the book, along with stories inspired by the book. There is also a profile section dedicated to the author of the original book and an interactive map showing other schools near you reading the same book. In the Factory, children can get inspired with various activities based on particular books. Users can choose from a menu of options relating to the book's title, author and the activity they want to participate in. The activity may be to draw or make or write a story. If users select 'draw', they will be taken to a page with colouring sheets and drawing challenges relating to the book. If they select 'make', they are taken to a page full of activity sheets and multimedia activity resources relating to the book. For example, for the book *Pirates!* by Deborah Allwright there is a video on 'how to create your own pirate adventure'. The Showroom is a collection of digital stories put together by individual children who have participated in the project. When you search by book title, you will find different children's interpretations of that book. The stories are presented in the form of texts and pictures or pictures only and are grouped by the book title so as to provide an at-a-glance overview of diverse students' responses to individual books.

> http://www.pop-up-hub.com/

Storyweaver

I mentioned Storyweaver in relation to its existing bank of resources in Chapter 9. The platform has grown into a database of some 2,000 books contributed by professional authors, as well as of illustrators and the online community members. The books are all richly illustrated and can be accessed on any device. In addition to fiction, there are non-fiction books on science and mathematics topics. Given that all the books are available under the Creative Commons licence, users can modify them and create new stories based on existing illustrations or text. Users can add their own translations to the original text and create completely new stories using the 'create' engine: they can add their own text to one of the Storyweaver illustrations or they can use pre-established templates. Finished stories can be printed out on A4 paper or saved as a digital story in the EPUB format. Moreover, users can submit their story to the community bank of stories and through the user dashboard authors can monitor how much their stories are liked and read by others. There are also video-based tutorials to help you create a story:

https://storyweaver.org.in/tutorials

Magic Blox

Magic Blox is an example of a digital library system that includes digital books written by award-winning authors as well as contributed by small independent publishers and the users themselves. The e-books on the site can be read on any device. This is a great example of how a community of readers and writers can come together in one virtual story space.

The site offers a special pricing programme for schools interested in using the digital library and also a revenue-share model for users who contribute their own content to the site. The latter is based on the number of times a book is read, and employs transparent reporting tools.

http://magicblox.com/

KidPub

KidPub started in 1995, which makes it one of the oldest ongoing reading platforms for young children. The site is both a library and a publishing site for digital books created by children for children. The platform claims to receive over a thousand new stories by children every month. Although the reading of the digital books is free, the contribution of titles requires a small fee (mostly for age verification purposes). Schools can subscribe to the site using the KidPub Press and parents can sign up their children by paying a nominal membership fee. Community elements include the facility to comment on stories, leave notes for other users or participate in writing contests. There is also the option to add to a 'never-ending story' that is unfolding with members' contributions. The platform works best on PCs and is heavily text based, so more suitable for older primary-school children.

https://www.kidpub.com/

Writing.com

Writing.com is a large online community of writers who can add their own multimedia stories to the site and read those contributed by other members. The site has been around since 2000 and is steadily growing its membership base. A lot of guidance is provided for the creation process, which encourages independent authorship. Children can choose what type of content they want to contribute to the site, with basic templates available for short stories but also for novels, essays, poems or even crossword puzzles. Users typically create their stories in text with one or two illustrations. Reviews of existing content are rewarded and crowd-sourced within the online community with a system of 'gift points'. The site is moderated (according to the website it has 80 moderators) and is primarily used by older children (lower secondary school).

https://www.writing.com/

Stories of a Lifetime

Stories of a Lifetime is a project set up by two UK teachers from Nottingham. They host and curate a website to which teachers from anywhere in the world can submit digital stories created with children in their classes. The site is particularly oriented towards video-based stories with minimal text.

http://jmilnereducation.wixsite.com/storiesofalifetime

Physical story places

In addition to projects that connect digital stories to physical objects, or that join up digital stories with living communities, there are organisations that link stories with physical places – rare and special places conducive to nurturing children's stories. Teachers, parents and librarians can participate in professional development training offered by these organisations or they can organise trips to visit the places with their classes. My favourite 'story places' are briefly described below.

The Ministry of Stories

The Ministry of Stories is 'a writing and mentoring space for young people aged 8–18', located in east London. The space offers programmes of story-writing workshops and one-to-one mentoring sessions with volunteer writing mentors. Besides its physical presence in London and diverse activities, the website of the Ministry of Stories contains a databank of teaching resources relating to poetry, letter writing and other story-inspiring activities. The programme of the writing workshops is linked to the England and Wales national curriculum and is strongly oriented towards supporting children's creativity, confidence and authorship through the process of producing written and illustrated physical books. Although the core of workshopping activities happens face to face in London, the website can be inspirational worldwide. Similar places can be found across the world; indeed the Ministry of Stories was inspired by 826 Valencia in San Francisco.

http://www.ministryofstories.org/

The Story Museum

The Story Museum is an international centre celebrating stories with events, workshops and exhibitions, based in Oxford. UK schools may be interested in participating in professional development training and outreach activities offered by the Story Museum. Its website hosts a database of audio-based stories, which can be searched by theme, origin, age group or keywords. The story text is available with the audio version of each story. The database is available from this link and can be listened to via any device with an internet connection:

http://www.storymuseum.org.uk/1001stories/

UK literacy charities

In addition to these unique story-related organisations, the UK has four fantastic literacy-related charities that work in close partnership with schools and parents to support children's story-making and story creation. The charities offer professional development training to teachers and librarians and their websites are packed with useful resources for anyone interested in literacy, including regular competitions for children and schools, story reviews, tips for parents and resources for educators. There are several literacy charities in the UK but these four have a strong digital presence with useful information for any English-speaking community.

Book Trust
https://www.booktrust.org.uk/

United Kingdom Literacy Association
https://ukla.org/

National Literacy Trust
https://literacytrust.org.uk/

The Reading Agency
https://readingagency.org.uk/

The Empathy Lab

It is also worth checking the work of and resources recommended by the Empathy Lab, which focuses on stories linked to empathy and on encouraging empathy among children and story authors.
        http://www.empathylab.uk/

Chapter summary

This chapter has provided some insights into the latest developments in the field of children's digital stories, with the aim of raising awareness about children's smart toys and tangibles. Examples of how these smart learning resources can be harnessed for educational use in the classroom were provided by drawing on some recent university-led innovation research projects. Digital story hubs and physical story spaces provide exciting and inspirational ideas for ways in which stories can connect to local and international communities. There is something in the future-gazing potential of these developments, particularly if the future gazing is put into the agency/reciprocity framework discussed in this book.

Reflection point

> There is no greater agony than bearing an untold story inside you. (Maya Angelou)

I hope that as you reach the end of this book and read this quote you will feel an urgency to share your story with the children and adults around you. Whether you decide to share your story in a multimedia or a print format does not matter. What matters is that you are aware of the possibilities of creating and sharing stories in the digital age and make discerned choices about how you support others to share their stories and how you share the 'untold story inside you'.

Further reading

Given that this is the last box of further reading in this book, I recommend here some books that touch on the broader topic of stories and technologies in children's lives and include ideas about important future developments in the area of children's digital literacies.

Erstad, O., Gilje, Ø., Sefton-Green, J. & Arnseth, H. C. (2016) *Learning Identities, Education and Community: Young Lives in the Cosmopolitan City*. Cambridge: Cambridge University Press.

Kucirkova, N., Rowsell, J. & Falloon, G. (eds) (2019) *The Routledge International Handbook of Playing and Learning with Technology in Early Childhood*. London: Routledge.

Livingstone, S. & Sefton-Green, J. (2016) *The Class: Living and Learning in the Digital Age*. New York: New York University Press.

Resnick, M. (2017). *Lifelong Kindergarten: Cultivating Creativity through Projects, Passion, Peers and Play*. Cambridge, MA: MIT Press.

Conclusion

You have reached the end of this book but I hope you do not feel it is finished. I have tried to structure this book as an ongoing journey that needs to be completed by other people. If you come across inspirational practices, resources or studies in this area and would like to share them with others please get in touch with me.

An important characteristic of children's reading on screen, which I hope I have conveyed through this book, is its personalised aspect. We all can be authors of children's digital books and personalise what they read and what we read with them. Children and their parents, teachers and other caring adults can create a digital book for and with other children in their class. Through this, the quality and value of children's digital books will be gradually increased. This process needs to be agentic and reciprocal to ensure that the 'personalisation' is not a tokenistic buzzword but a genuine and felt experience for everyone involved.

Digital books are an integral part of children's contemporary reading practices; this book aims to raise awareness of their potential as well as their current limitations. With an underpinning that reading is a social practice, I have foregrounded shared and communal uses of digital books, ranging from one-to-one adult–child reading at home to buddy reading at school and international online reading hubs.

With various children's smartphone and tablet apps, teachers can make books for and with children, practising vital literacy skills and learning together with and about each other. With multimodal story-making apps, teachers can add not only texts and pictures but also sounds to accompany their stories. The digital format allows teachers to update their stories periodically and flexibly, breaking away from the rigidity of the traditional print format. A collaborative story-making process is likely to be followed by joint story-sharing, a unique part of the story cycle. I hope that the suggestions, tips and examples in this book will empower you to try to experience this cycle.

I have been fortunate to observe how authoring stories empowers families and fosters a space where unclaimed identities can be celebrated. Parents and caregivers too can be authors of digital books and engage in story authorship for or with their children. The digital format can facilitate the expression of meaning in various modes and the distribution of stories among various language and culture groups. The importance of dialogue and the child's own agency in accessing and enjoying stories needs to be taken into account when discussing and facilitating the use of children's digital books. Children's active participation is a key driver for many publishers and producers of story-making apps, resources and spaces. The processes of story-making and story-sharing can be acts of active vocalisation of one's life story.

To conclude, stories are an essential dynamic of life, and digital technologies can grant them posterity, discoverability and geographical advantage. The world of children's digital stories is growing exponentially; large community platforms are crowdsourcing and curating multimedia stories, and smart toys are interconnecting virtual and physical story worlds. The future will be bright if we allow stories to be the universal force that binds diverse communities, calls forth agency in adults and children and accounts for the complementarity between physical and virtual spaces.

References

AAP Committee on Public Education (1999) 'Media education', *Pediatrics*, 104(2, pt 1): 341–3.

AAP Council on Communications and Media (2011) 'Media use by children younger than 2 years', *Pediatrics*, 128(5): 1040–5.

AAP Council on Communications and Media (2016) 'Media and young minds', *Pediatrics*, 138(5). http://pediatrics.aappublications.org/content/138/5/e20162591.full

Adams, J. (1961) *Diary and Autobiography*, Vol. 3. Cambridge, MA: Belknap Press of Harvard University Press.

Aghlara, L. & Tamjid, N. H. (2011) 'The effect of digital games on Iranian children's vocabulary retention in foreign language acquisition', *Procedia – Social and Behavioral Sciences*, 29: 552–60.

Aliagas, C. & Margallo, A. M. (2017) 'Children's responses to the interactivity of storybook apps in family shared reading events involving the iPad', *Literacy*, 51(1): 44–52.

Baron, N. S. (2015) *Words Onscreen: The Fate of Reading in a Digital World*. Oxford: Oxford University Press.

Barrs, M. & Horrocks, S. (2014) *Educational Blogs and Their Effects on Pupils' Writing*. Reading: CfBT Education Trust.

Bearne, E., Dombey, H. & Grainger, T. (2003) *Classroom Interactions in Literacy*. Maidenhead: McGraw-Hill.

Bernhard, J. K., Winsler, A., Bleiker, C., Ginieniewicz, J. & Madigan, A. L. (2008) '"Read my story!" Using the early authors program to promote early literacy among diverse, urban preschool children in poverty', *Journal of Education for Students Placed at Risk*, 13(1): 76–105.

Brinton, D. M., Kagan, O. & Bauckus, S. (2017) *Heritage Language Education: A New Field Emerging*. London: Routledge.

Broadbent, H., Fell, L., Green, P. & Gardner, W. (2013) *Have Your Say: Listening to Young People about Their Online Rights and Responsibilities*. Plymouth: Childnet International and UK Safer Internet Centre.

Brueck, J. S. & Lenhart, L. A. (2015) 'E-books and TPACK', *The Reading Teacher*, 68(5): 373–6.

Bruner, J. S. (2003) *Making Stories: Law, Literature, Life*. Cambridge, MA: Harvard University Press.

Bruner, J. S. (2009) *Actual Minds, Possible Worlds*. Cambridge, MA: Harvard University Press.

Burnett, C. (2014) 'Investigating pupils' interactions around digital texts: a spatial perspective on the "classroom-ness" of digital literacy practices in schools', *Educational Review*, 66(2): 192–209.

Burnett, C. (2016) *The Digital Age and Its Implications for Learning and Teaching in the Primary School*. York: Cambridge Primary Review Trust.

Burnett, C. & Merchant, G. (2017) 'The case of the iPad', in *The Case of the iPad*, edited by C. Burnett, G. Merchant, A. Simpson & M. Walsh, 1–14. Singapore: Springer.

Calvert, S. L. (2008) 'Children as consumers: advertising and marketing', *The Future of Children*, 18(1): 205–234.

Christ, T., Wang, X. C. & Erdemir, E. (2018) 'Young children's buddy reading with multimodal app books: reading patterns and characteristics of readers, texts, and contexts', *Early Child Development and Care*, 188(8): 1012–30.

Clapp, E. P., Ross, J., Ryan, J. O. & Tishman, S. (2016) *Maker-Centered Learning: Empowering Young People to Shape Their Worlds*. London: John Wiley.

Common Sense Media (2016) 'The common sense census: plugged-in parents of tweens and teens 2016'. https://www.commonsensemedia.org/research/the-common-sense-census-plugged-in-parents-of-tweens-and-teens-2016

Cremin, T. (2016) 'Reading: re-asserting the potency of the personal', Cambridge Primary Review Trust. https://cprtrust.org.uk/cprt-blog/reading-re-asserting-the-potency-of-the-personal

Cremin, T., Mottram, M., Collins, F., Powell, S. & Safford, K. (2009) 'Teachers as readers: building communities of readers', *Literacy*, 43(1): 11–19.

Cremin, T., Mottram, M., Collins, F. M., Powell, S. & Safford, K. (2014) *Building Communities of Engaged Readers: Reading for Pleasure*. London: Routledge.

Cremin, T., Flewitt, R., Mardell, B. & Swann, J. (eds) (2016) *Storytelling in Early Childhood: Enriching Language, Literacy and Classroom Culture*. London: Taylor & Francis.

Cummins, J. (2005) 'A proposal for action: strategies for recognizing heritage language competence as a learning resource within the mainstream classroom', *Modern Language Journal*, 89(4): 585–92.

Curenton, S. M., Craig, M. J. & Flanigan, N. (2008) 'Use of decontextualized talk across story contexts: how oral storytelling and emergent reading can scaffold children's development', *Early Education and Development*, 19(1): 161–87.

De Jong, M. T. & Bus, A. G. (2002) 'Quality of book-reading matters for emergent readers: an experiment with the same book in a regular or electronic format', *Journal of Educational Psychology*, 94(1): 145–55.

DeMoulin, D. F. (2001) 'The hidden value of personalization and rhyme in reading', *Reading Improvement*, 38(3): 116–19.

Dezuanni, M., Dooley, K., Gattenhof, S. & Knight, L. (2015) *iPads in the Early Years: Developing Literacy and Creativity*. New York: Routledge.

Donohue, C. (ed.) (2014) *Technology and Digital Media in the Early Years: Tools for Teaching and Learning*. New York: Routledge.

Druin, A. (2005) 'What children can teach us: developing digital libraries for children with children', *Library Quarterly*, 75(1): 20–41.

Druin, A., Bederson, B. B., Weeks, A., Farber, A., Grosjean, J., Guha, M. L., Hourcade, J. P., Lee, J., Liao, K., Reuter, K., Rose, A., Takayama, Y. & Zhang, L. (2003) 'The International Children's Digital Library: description and analysis of first use', Human–Computer Interaction Laboratory, University of Maryland. http://www.cs.umd.edu/hcil/trs/2003-02/2003-02.pdf

Engel de Abreu, P. M., Cruz-Santos, A., Tourinho, C. J., Martin, R. & Bialystok, E. (2012) 'Bilingualism enriches the poor: enhanced cognitive control in low-income minority children', *Psychological Science*, 23(11): 1364–71.

Erstad, O., Gilje, Ø., Sefton-Green, J. & Arnseth, H. C. (2016) *Learning Identities, Education and Community: Young Lives in the Cosmopolitan City*. Cambridge: Cambridge University Press.

Garbe, C., Lafontaine, D., Shiel, G., Sulkunen, S., Valtin, R., Baye, A. & Géron, S. (2016) 'Literacy in Finland. Country report. Children and adolescents'. http://www.eli-net.eu/fileadmin/ELINET/Redaktion/user_upload/Finland_Short_Report.pdf

Golding, K. (2014) *Using Stories to Build Bridges with Traumatized Children: Creative Ideas for Therapy, Life Story Work, Direct Work and Parenting*. London: Jessica Kingsley.

González, N., Moll, L. C. & Amanti, C. (2006) *Funds of Knowledge: Theorizing Practices in Households, Communities, and Classrooms*. New York: Routledge.

Goodwin, P. (ed.) (2017) *The Literate Classroom*. London: Routledge.

Guernsey, L. & Levine, M. H. (2015) *Tap, Click, Read: Growing Readers in a World of Screens*. New York: John Wiley.

Hague, C. & Williamson, B. (2009) *Digital Participation, Digital Literacy, and School Subjects: A Review of the Policies, Literature and Evidence*. London: Futurelab. https://www.nfer.ac.uk/digital-participation-digital-literacy-and-school-subjects-a-review-of-the-policies-literature-and-evidence

Heafner, T. L. (2014) 'Exploring the effectiveness of online education in K-12 environments', IGI Global. https://www.amazon.co.uk/Exploring-Effectiveness-Education-Environments-Childhood/dp/1466663839

Heydon, R. M. (2005) 'The de-pathologization of childhood, disability and aging in an intergenerational art class: implications for educators', *Journal of Early Childhood Research*, 3(3): 243–68.

Heydon, R. M. (2007) 'Making meaning together: multi-modal literacy learning opportunities in an inter-generational art programme', *Journal of Curriculum Studies*, 39(1): 35–62.

Hoel, T. & Mason, J. (2018) 'Standards for smart education – towards a development framework', *Smart Learning Environments*, 5(1). https://link.springer.com/article/10.1186/s40561-018-0052-3

Hunt, P. (2000) 'Futures for children's literature: evolution or radical break?', *Cambridge Journal of Education*, 30(1): 111–19.

Ihamäki, P. & Heljakka, K. (2017) 'Workshop on the internet of toys: character toys with digital dimensions and connections', paper presented at the 21st International Academic Mindtrek Conference, Tampere, 20–1 September.

Janes, H. & Kermani, H. (2001) 'Caregivers' story reading to young children in family literacy programs: pleasure or punishment?', *Journal of Adolescent & Adult Literacy*, 44(5): 458–66.

Johnston, P. H. (2004) *Choice Words: How Our Language Affects Children's Learning*. Portland, ME: Stenhouse.

Kabali, H. K., Irigoyen, M. M., Nunez-Davis, R., Budacki, J. G., Mohanty, S. H., Leister, K. P. & Bonner, R. L. (2015) 'Exposure and use of mobile media devices by young children', *Pediatrics*, 136(6): 1044–50.

Kiousis, S. (2002) 'Interactivity: a concept explication', *New Media & Society*, 4(3): 355–83.

Kucirkova, N. (2014a) 'How to be a publishing parent – and help diversify children's literature', *The Conversation*, 2 July. https://theconversation.com/how-to-be-a-publishing-parent-and-help-diversify-childrens-literature-28744

Kucirkova, N. (2014b) *iPads and Tablets in the Classroom: Personalising Children's Stories*. Leicester: UKLA.

Kucirkova, N. (2014c) 'Kindle vs ebooks? Children just don't see it that way', *The Conversation*, 18 April. https://theconversation.com/kindle-vs-books-children-just-dont-see-it-that-way-25725

Kucirkova, N. (2014d) 'Shiny appy children', *The Guardian*, 15 December. https://www.theguardian.com/science/head-quarters/2014/dec/15/shiny-appy-children

Kucirkova, N.(2015a) 'Confused by the mysterious world of children's digital books?', *Huffington Post*, 27 July. https://www.huffingtonpost.co.uk/dr-natalia-kucirkova/childrens-digital-books_b_7825836.html

Kucirkova, N. (2015b) 'Personalised books: exciting but also risky times for children's stories', *Huffington Post*, 22 September. https://www.huffingtonpost.co.uk/dr-natalia-kucirkova/personalised-books_b_8167436.html

Kucirkova, N. (2015c) 'Story-making with iPad apps: baking stories in the 21st century', *Exchange*, March/April, 43–6. https://www.childcareexchange.com/catalog/magazine/

Kucirkova, N. (2016a) 'Digital personal stories: bringing together generations and enriching communities', in *Literacy, Media and Technology: Past, Present and Future*, edited by C. Burnett, G. Merchant & B. Parry, 129–43. London: Bloomsbury.

Kucirkova, N. (2016b) 'Personalisation: a theoretical possibility to reinvigorate children's interest in storybook reading and facilitate greater book diversity', *Contemporary Issues in Early Childhood*, 17(3): 1–16.

Kucirkova, N. (2017a) 'Children's reading on screen: in the beginning was the word, not a hotspot', *The Guardian*, 4 December. https://www.theguardian.com/education/head-quarters/2017/dec/04/childrens-reading-on-screen-in-the-beginning-was-the-word-not-a-hotspot

Kucirkova, N. (2017b) *Digital Personalization in Early Childhood: Impact on Childhood*. London: Bloomsbury.

Kucirkova, N. (2017c) 'How can digital personal(ized) books enrich the language arts curriculum?', *Reading Teacher*, 71(3): 275–84.

Kucirkova, N. (2017d) 'iRPD – a framework for guiding design-based research for iPad apps', *British Journal of Educational Technology*, 48(2): 598–610.

Kucirkova, N. & Cremin, T. (2017) 'Personalised reading for pleasure with digital libraries: towards a pedagogy of practice and design', *Cambridge Journal of Education*, 25 September. https://doi.org/10.1080/0305764X.2017.1375458

Kucirkova, N. & Cremin, T. (forthcoming) *Children Reading for Pleasure in the Digital Age*. London: SAGE.

Kucirkova, N. & Falloon, G. (2016) *Apps, Technology and Younger Learners: International Evidence for Teaching*. London: Taylor & Francis.

Kucirkova, N. & Littleton, K. (2016) *The Digital Reading Habits of Children: A National Survey of Parents' Perceptions of and Practices in Relation to Children's Reading for Pleasure with Print and Digital Books*. London: Book Trust.

Kucirkova, N. & Littleton K. (2017) 'Developing personalised education for personal mobile technologies with the pluralisation agenda', *Oxford Review of Education*, 43(3): 276–88.

Kucirkova, N. & Quinlan, O. (eds) (2017) *The Digitally Agile Researcher*. London: McGraw-Hill.

Kucirkova, N. & Sakr, M. (2015) 'Child–father creative text-making at home with crayons, iPad collage & PC', *Thinking Skills and Creativity*, 17: 59–73.

Kucirkova, N. & Zuckerman, B. (2017) 'A guiding framework for considering touchscreens in children under two', *International Journal of Child–Computer Interaction*, 12(C): 46–9.

Kucirkova, N., Messer, D., Sheehy, K. & Flewitt, R. (2013) 'Sharing personalised stories on iPads: a close look at one parent–child interaction', *Literacy*, 47(3): 115–22.

Kucirkova, N., Messer, D. & Sheehy, K. (2014a) 'The effects of personalisation on young children's spontaneous speech during shared book reading', *Journal of Pragmatics*, 71: 45–55.

Kucirkova, N., Messer, D. & Sheehy, K. (2014b) 'Reading personalized books with preschool children enhances their word acquisition', *First Language*, 34(3): 227–43.

Kucirkova, N., Messer, D., Critten, V. & Harwood, J. (2014c) 'Story-making on the iPad when children have complex needs: two case studies', *Communication Disorders Quarterly*, 36(1): 44–54.

Kucirkova, N., Ng, I. & Holtby, J. (2017a) *From Mirrors to Selfies: Protecting Children's Data for Personalised Learning and Future Growth*. London: University College of London, Institute of Education.

Kucirkova, N., Sheehy, K. & Messer, D. (2015) 'A Vygotskian perspective on parent–child talk during iPad story sharing', *Journal of Research in Reading*, 38(4): 428-441.

Kucirkova, N., Snow, C. E., Grøver, V. & McBride, C. (eds) (2017b) *The Routledge International Handbook of Early Literacy Education: A Contemporary Guide to Literacy Teaching and Interventions in a Global Context*. London: Taylor & Francis.

Kucirkova, N., Rowsell, J. & Falloon, G. (eds) (in press) *The Routledge International Handbook of Playing and Learning with Technology in Early Childhood*. London: Routledge.

Leander, K. M. & Sheehy, M. (2004) *Spatializing Literacy Research and Practice*. New York: Peter Lang.

Lee, T. (2015) *Princesses, Dragons and Helicopter Stories: Storytelling and Story Acting in the Early Years*. London: Routledge.

Livingstone, S. & Sefton-Green, J. (2016) *The Class: Living and Learning in the Digital Age*. New York: New York University Press.

McCannon, D., Thornton, S. & Williams, Y. (2008) *The Encyclopedia of Writing and Illustrating Children's Books: From Creating Characters to Developing Stories, a Step-by-Step Guide to Making Magical Picture Books*. Philadelphia: Allen & Unwin.

McClure, M. A. (2007) 'Building theories: play, making, and pedagogical documentation in early childhood art education', PhD dissertation, Pennsylvania State University.

Mathew Myers, J. & Halpin, R. (2002) 'Teachers' attitudes and use of multimedia technology in the classroom: constructivist-based professional development training for school districts', *Journal of Computing in Teacher Education*, 18(4): 133–40.

Mercer, N. & Littleton, K. (2007) *Dialogue and the Development of Children's Thinking: A Sociocultural Approach*. London: Routledge.

Mishra, P. & Koehler, M. J. (2006) 'Technological pedagogical content knowledge: a framework for teacher knowledge', *Teachers College Record*, 108(6): 1017–1054.

Moll, L. C. (1992) 'Bilingual classroom studies and community analysis: some recent trends', *Educational Researcher*, 21(2): 20–4.

Moll, L. C., Amanti, C., Neff, D. & Gonzalez, N. (1992) 'Funds of knowledge for teaching: using a qualitative approach to connect homes and classrooms', *Theory into Practice*, 31(2): 132–41.

National Literacy Trust (2016) 'Celebrating reading for enjoyment: findings from our Annual Literacy Survey 2016 report'. https://literacytrust.org.uk/research-services/research-reports/celebrating-reading-enjoyment-findings-our-annual-literacy-survey-2016-report/

Neuburger, E. K. (2012) *Show Me a Story: 40 Craft Projects and Activities to Spark Children's Storytelling*. North Adams, MA: Storey.

Oakley, G., Howitt, C., Garwood, R. & Durack, A.-R. (2013) 'Becoming multimodal authors: pre-service teachers' interventions to support young children with autism', *Australasian Journal of Early Childhood*, 38(3): 20–24.

Ok, M. W., Kim, M. K., Kang, E. Y. & Bryant, B. R. (2016) 'How to find good apps: an evaluation rubric for instructional apps for teaching students with learning disabilities', *Intervention in School and Clinic*, 51(4): 244–52.

Oulasvirta, A. & Blom, J. (2008) 'Motivations in personalisation behaviour', *Interacting with Computers*, 20(1): 1–16.

Pahl, K. & Rowsell, J. (2010) *Artifactual Literacies: Every Object Tells a Story*. New York: Teachers College Press.

Parish-Morris, J., Mahajan, N., Hirsh-Pasek, K., Golinkoff, R. M. & Collins, M. F. (2013) 'Once upon a time: parent–child dialogue and storybook reading in the electronic era', *Mind, Brain, and Education*, 7(3): 200–11.

Parry, B., Burnett, C. & Merchant, G. (eds) (2016) *Literacy, Media, Technology: Past, Present and Future*. London: Bloomsbury.

Picton, I. (2014) *The Impact of Ebooks on the Reading Motivation and Reading Skills of Children and Young People: A Rapid Literature Review*. London: National Literacy Trust.

Picton, I. & Clark, C. (2015) 'The impact of ebooks on the reading motivation and reading skills of children and young people: a study of schools using RM Books', final report, National Literacy Trust.

Poarch, G. J. & van Hell, J. G. (2012) 'Executive functions and inhibitory control in multilingual children: evidence from second-language learners, bilinguals, and trilinguals', *Journal of Experimental Child Psychology*, 113(4): 535–51.

Potter, J. (2012) *Digital Media and Learner Identity: The New Curatorship*. London: Springer.

Prensky, M. (2001) 'Digital natives, digital immigrants part 1', *On the Horizon*, 9(5): 1–6.

Prior, J. & Van Herwegen, J. (eds) (2016) *Practical Research with Children*. London: Routledge.

Quinlan, O. (2013) *The Thinking Teacher*. Carmarthen: Crown House.

Ramdarshan Bold, M. (2018) 'The eight percent problem: authors of colour in the British young adult market (2006–2016)', *Publishing Research Quarterly*, 34: 385–46.

Reese, E. (2012) 'The tyranny of shared book-reading', in *Contemporary Debates in Childhood Education and Development*, edited by S. Suggate & E. Reese, 59–68. New York: Routledge.

Remington, A. & Fairnie, J. (2017) 'A sound advantage: increased auditory capacity in autism', *Cognition*, 166: 459–65.

Resnick, M. (2017) *Lifelong Kindergarten: Cultivating Creativity through Projects, Passion, Peers and Play*. Cambridge, MA: MIT Press.

Roberts-Mahoney, H., Means, A. J. & Garrison, M. J. (2016) 'Netflixing human capital development: personalized learning technology and the corporatization of K-12 education', *Journal of Education Policy*, 31(4): 405–20.

Roskos, K., Burstein, K. & You, B.-K. (2012) 'A typology for observing children's engagement with ebooks at preschool', *Journal of Interactive Online Learning*, 11(2). http://www.ncolr.org/jiol/issues/pdf/11.2.1.pdf

Rowe, L. W. (2018) 'Say it in your language: supporting translanguaging in multilingual classes', *Reading Teacher*, 5 January. https://doi.org/10.1002/trtr.1673

Sakr, M., Federici, R., Hall, N., Trivedy, B. & O'Brien, L. (2018) *Creativity and Making in Early Childhood*. London: Bloomsbury.

Salmon, G. (2002) *E-tivities: The Key to Active Online Learning*, London: Kogan Page.

Salmon, G. (2011) *E-moderating: The Key to Teaching and Learning Online*. New York: Routledge.

Sari, B., Takacs, Z. K. & Bus, A. G. (2017) 'What are we downloading for our children? Best-selling children's apps in four European countries', *Journal of Early Childhood Literacy*, 14 December. https://doi.org/10.1177/1468798417744057

Sefton-Green, J., Marsh, J., Erstad, O. & Flewitt, R. (2016) 'Establishing a research agenda for the digital literacy practices of young children', White Paper, COST Action IS1410. http://digilitey.eu/wp-content/uploads/2015/09/DigiLitEYWP.pdf

Segal-Drori, O., Korat, O., Shamir, A. & Klein, P. S. (2010) 'Reading electronic and printed books with and without adult instruction: effects on emergent reading', *Reading and Writing*, 23(8): 913–30.

Shabat, A. & Korat, O. (2017) 'Background music and content expansion support story comprehension in e-book reading of preschoolers', paper presented at DigiLitEy Conference, Bologna, 31 August to 1 September. http://digilitey.eu/wp-content/uploads/2015/09/Background-Music-and-Content-Expansion.pdf

Sheehy, K. & Holliman, A. (eds) (2017) *Education and New Technologies: Perils and Promises for Learners*. London: Routledge.

Smeets, D. J. & Bus, A. G. (2012) 'Interactive electronic storybooks for kindergartners to promote vocabulary growth', *Journal of Experimental Child Psychology*, 112(1): 36–55.

Snow, C. (2002) *Reading for Understanding: Toward an R&D Program in Reading Comprehension*. Santa Monica, CA: Rand.

Sung, H.-Y. & Siraj-Blatchford, J. (2014) 'Adults and children creating personalised stories together through information and communications technology in public libraries', paper presented at Libraries, Citizens, Societies: Confluence for Knowledge, Lyons, 16–22 August.

Taylor, E. & Michael, K. (2016) 'Smart toys that are the stuff of nightmares', *IEEE Technology and Society Magazine*, 35(1): 8–10.

Turvey, K., Potter, J., Burton, J., Allen, J. & Sharp, J. (2016) *Primary Computing and Digital Technologies: Knowledge, Understanding and Practice*. London: SAGE.

Unsworth, L. (2006) *E-literature for Children: Enhancing Digital Literacy Learning*. New York: Taylor & Francis.

Vaala, S., Ly, A. & Levine, M. H. (2015) 'Getting a read on the app stores: a market scan and analysis of children's literacy apps. Full report', Joan Ganz Cooney Center at Sesame Workshop, New York. http://www.joanganzcooneycenter.org/wp-content/uploads/2015/12/jgcc_gettingaread.pdf

Verhallen, M. J. & Bus, A. G. (2010) 'Low-income immigrant pupils learning vocabulary through digital picture storybooks', *Journal of Educational Psychology*, 102(1): 54–61.

Walker, H., Kucirkova, N. & Gould, R. (2016) 'UKLA Digital Book Award: teachers' perceptions of the winning apps in 2015', *English 4–11*, 57: 19–21.

Walker, E., Adams, A., Restrepo, M. A., Fialko, S. & Glenberg, A. M. (2017) 'When (and how) interacting with technology-enhanced storybooks helps dual language learners', *Translational Issues in Psychological Science*, 3(1): 66–79.

Williams, M. (2014) 'How to encourage students to read for pleasure: teachers share their top tips', *The Guardian*, 3 June. https://www.theguardian.com/teacher-network/teacher-blog/2014/jun/03/how-to-encourage-students-read-for-pleasure-teacher-top-tips

Wohlwend, K. E. (2015) 'One screen, many fingers: young children's collaborative literacy play with digital puppetry apps and touchscreen technologies', *Theory into Practice*, 54(2): 154–62.

Wolf, M. (2007) *Proust and the Squid: The Story and Science of the Reading Brain*. New York: HarperCollins.

Wolf, M. (2018) Reader, Come Home: The Fate of the Reading Brain in a Digital World. New York: HarperCollins.

Young, R. & Ferguson, P. (2018) 'A guide to reading with young children', Literacy for Pleasure. https://literacyforpleasure.files.wordpress.com/2018/03/a-guide-to-reading-with-children.pdf

Zeichner, K. and Liu, K. (2010) 'A critical analysis of reflection as a goal for teacher education', in *Handbook of Reflection and Reflective Inquiry: Mapping a Way of Knowing for Professional Reflective Inquiry*, edited by N. Lyons, 67–83. New York: Springer.

Index

Lightning Source UK Ltd.
Milton Keynes UK
UKHW021512101218
333767UK00004B/398/P